THE
KELAYRES
MASSACRE

For "Amtrak" Ron -

Stephanie Hoover

Oct. 2014

THE
KELAYRES
MASSACRE

POLITICS & MURDER IN PENNSYLVANIA'S ANTHRACITE COAL COUNTRY

STEPHANIE HOOVER

THE
History
PRESS

Published by The History Press
Charleston, SC 29403
www.historypress.net

Copyright © 2014 by Stephanie Hoover
All rights reserved

First published 2014

Manufactured in the United States

ISBN 978.1.62619.547.9

Library of Congress CIP data applied for.

To my mother, Marian, who loves a good book.
(Here's another one.)

CONTENTS

Acknowledgements   9
Introduction   13

1. Miners, Strikers and State Police   17
2. Bootlegging, Drinking and Gambling   23
3. The Bruno Family   29
4. Seeds of a Revolt   33
5. The McAloose Faction   37
6. A Parade Ends in Bloodshed   39
7. The Election of 1934   51
8. The Funerals   55
9. Prisoner Joseph J. Bruno   59
10. The Trials   63
11. The Legend of Lewis Buono Begins   79
12. Joe Checks Out of the Bruno Hotel   83
13. Anatomy of an Escape   89
14. Frank Miller Comes Home   95
15. The Aftermath   101
16. Around in a Circle   109

Sources   113
Index   119
About the Author   123

ACKNOWLEDGEMENTS

The most wonderful thing about writing a book about events occurring in the twentieth century (as opposed to my two earlier books, both of which were set in the late 1800s) is that you get to speak to real, live human beings. Children. Grandchildren. Nieces and nephews. Others who wrote about and researched the events. Even those whose family members investigated and prosecuted the accused. And all of these examples actually happened as I was researching *The Kelayres Massacre: Politics & Murder in Pennsylvania's Anthracite Coal Country.*

First and foremost, I must thank Lucille Trella, a little sparkplug of a lady and the current owner of Joe Bruno's home in Kelayres. Lucille has no reservations about living in the house from which most of the shooting took place. It is not *her* history, after all—it is just *history*. But that doesn't mean she's not in some way the curator of it. Many folks have stopped and knocked on her door—some doing historical research, others researching their family histories. And Lucille greets them all, happily sharing what she knows about the Brunos and the home "Big Joe" built, all served with a wonderful side dish of pictures of her own children and grandchildren. If you're lucky enough to meet Lucille, just sit back and enjoy the ride. I did.

Catty-corner across the street from Lucille is the gray brick home of Paul Salidago. Like Lucille's, Paul's home is permanently tied to the Kelayres Massacre and still bears the scars from bullets that penetrated its side. Unlike Lucille, Paul has a personal attachment to the massacre: his uncle was shot during the mêlée and died some months later. And it was in the second-floor apartment that one of the accused perpetrators of the massacre lived. In one of those puzzling twists of fate, it was also into the Salidagos' former drugstore, looking out over the deadly intersection, that one of the victims was dragged. Paul showed me the spot, and I could only imagine while standing in it that he has pondered the events of November 5, 1934, more than any other living soul.

Deborah Bruno Motika, granddaughter of Joe Bruno, agreed to speak to me—and I am forever amazed and thankful for it. Not surprising, Deb holds a more forgiving and favorable view of Joe. Like Paul Salidago, she possesses and carries a piece of the surviving, living DNA of the Kelayres Massacre. She never met her grandfather, but she grew up hearing the stories told by his children—including Joe's youngest son, Ernest, her father. "I can't change what he did," Deb says of Joe's actions on that election eve eighty years ago. "I can't take responsibility for something that happened before I was born." But unlike her siblings, she has assumed the role of family historian, even traveling to New York to photograph the apartment building where Joe briefly holed up during his time on the run. And it was Deb who provided the wonderful portrait of Joe found in Chapter 4.

Of course, there is no crime without investigation, and my hat is off to the men (and today, women) of the Pennsylvania State Police. PSP historian Thomas Memmi was instrumental in creating for me the true picture of the firepower used and the damage inflicted in the massacre. He invited me to the academy in Hershey where a most grand discovery was made: the contents of an old display case dedicated to the Kelayres shootings. He and Sergeant Jeffery D. Zapach, in charge of the safekeeping of these archival gems, literally made parts of this book possible by presenting for my review actual, still-tagged evidence from the investigation and trials, including a victim's shoe (complete with through-and-through bullet holes), the pellet-riddled American flag held by one of the Democrats in the political parade and a man's tie so bloodstained that its original colors are hard to discern. Like a pair of criminal science Indiana Joneses, they brought these historical treasures forth from the deep and allowed me to both touch and photograph them.

And speaking of evidence collection, my first-ever posthumous acknowledgment goes to Lewis D. Buono—a man who made enforcing the law a lifelong passion. If there is a hero in this story, it is certainly this man. Buono's descendants—some of whom I communicated with during my research—should be proud of their "famous detective" forefather. Although the topic and scope of this book allowed only a brief overview of his exploits, his amazing career merits its own book-length treatment.

ACKNOWLEDGEMENTS

Another amazing find so instrumental to this book was a box of files donated to the Schuylkill County Historical Society by the county courthouse. Contents included depositions, maps and photos of the crime scene, pictures of the Bruno family, handwritten notes by Detective Buono and even bullets recovered from the scene. I had unfettered access to these items and returned twice to paw through them, all the while welcomed heartily by society staff.

There are so many other people and organizations to thank: librarians throughout the Schuylkill County library system who took time to answer my e-mails, family members who responded to my unexpected letters, repositories like the Pennsylvania State Archives (special thanks to Christina Stetler and Mary Fenton) that preserve and maintain such vital historical records and artifacts and, of course, my home away from home: the Pennsylvania State Library, where the indispensable Kathy Hale and Charlese Farmer treat me with far more respect than I'm entitled.

And last, but hardly least, I must thank my husband, son and mother, who serve as proofreaders, critics and cheerleaders—whichever might be necessary on any given day. The mistakes that might be found within my writing are mine. The suggestions that make my books as good as they can possibly be are theirs.

Even more than with my two previous books, I felt a personal and overwhelming obligation to honor those family members (gone or still here) who were forever impacted by the violent events of eight decades back. I hope they believe that I have.

INTRODUCTION

When it comes to American politics, perhaps the only thing we can all agree on is that we have become a bitter, divided and feuding society. Republicans refuse to accept that any aspect of liberalism might be of merit. Democrats refuse to believe their liberalism is not universally admired. Neither the politicians themselves nor their followers can ever discuss these differences rationally, it seems. There is no longer a civil debate with the good of the electorate at the center of it. Instead, many encounters between these presumably intelligent high-achievers descend into what resemble epic Jerry Springer episodes. When on the rare but shockingly real occasion these arguments turn physical, we try to *appear* appalled—but deep down, we're more than a little entertained. Because, after all, it's not like they're going to actually kill one another, right?

Wrong.

From the 1804 Burr-Hamilton duel to the 2013 murders of a Kaufman County, Texas district attorney and his wife, politics has always had a deadly side. What sets the Kelayres Massacre apart is the sheer enormity of the carnage—and the fact that so few people are aware that it even happened. It has, for the most part, escaped the attention of political historians. This is particularly strange when one considers that it was a national story, one that shared front-page, above-the-fold coverage with the Bruno Hauptmann trial in the *New York Times* and was covered by reporters from *Time* magazine.

Perhaps it is inconspicuous because it was overshadowed by an all-encompassing national quarrel. The United States was, at the time, embroiled in one of the most heated policy debate battles ever waged: whether to keep and affirm FDR's New Deal programs or reject and repeal them. By anyone's measure, Pennsylvania was a key state in both the 1932 and 1934 elections—what we now call a "swing state," one whose voting results could swing in favor of either party to great effect. All eyes were on the Keystone State that year. Would it, as during the 1932 presidential election, reject Roosevelt and his vast social programs? Or might it continue in its slow transition toward the philosophies of the Democrats and signal to the rest of the nation that Pennsylvania welcomed and validated FDR's liberal "big-spending" (said the conservatives) approach to invigorating the economy? It was a question that consumed far more ink, and invoked far more punditry, than the Kelayres Massacre ever would.

But while FDR's New Deal may have consumed the nation's interest—and the rest of the state's, for that matter—the disputes in Kelayres, Kline Township, Schuylkill County, were far more immediate and personal. The tiny coal town of fewer than eight hundred souls was making a more gut-level choice: whether to allow Republican political boss Joe Bruno and family to hold the positions of justice of the peace, school board member and tax collector. And voters made this decision with no small amount of resolve and fortitude, for "Big Joe" ran Kline Township and everyone knew it. He lent money for mortgages and provided alcohol, which up to exactly one year prior to the 1934 election was illegal to make or consume. The Brunos exerted influence over county commissioners and exhibited excessive generosity toward the only Italian American Catholic church in Kelayres. Joe Bruno was the closest thing to a king—or a Mario Puzo–style organized crime boss—the people of Kline Township would ever know.

Indeed, one of the most intriguing, and probably most inflated, aspects of the story of the Kelayres Massacre is the rumor that it has some tie to "organized crime." There are whispers that "Big Joe" Bruno was "mobbed up." If he was, there were no witnesses to attest to it.

Surely, Bruno must have known the reputations of some fellow Italian Americans in the area. Supposedly, the Amber Lantern Tavern in nearby Tamaqua served as a hangout for members of a Philadelphia outfit. The Scranton/Wilkes-Barre–based Bufalino crime family lived just a few miles north of Kelayres in Hazleton, a town dubbed "mob city" by newspapers. But was Bruno himself a key member of organized crime? He may have attempted to emulate mobsters' style and methods, but it appears Joe's interests were far too selfish to share with anyone outside his own blood family.

In true political fashion, both parties tried to spin the killing of five unarmed parade marchers (and injuries of dozens more) to their advantage. The Democrats viewed the horrifying event as part of a vast Republican conspiracy to frighten voters away from the polls. Hardly surprising, Bruno's Republicans described the parade marchers as an incensed Democrat mob who (according to their unsuccessful defense) hurled projectiles at the Bruno home, forcing its occupants to defend themselves against what they believed was an imminent and violent home invasion.

Even today, the true villains and heroes of the Kelayres Massacre are subject to debate by those who have heard the story from family members and neighbors. But regardless of loyalties and the passage of time, the tragic loss of life on November 5, 1934, can never be excused—nor can we casually write it off as a shocking but expected outcome in the dirty game of politics.

Like other tragedies, the Kelayres Massacre can and must be studied, analyzed and reported to ensure that it is never repeated. That's what this book sets out to do.

Chapter 1

MINERS, STRIKERS AND STATE POLICE

I n 1932, Franklin Delano Roosevelt won the presidential election by more than seven million votes. He did not, however, win Pennsylvania. In fact, of the meager fifty-nine electoral votes collected by Roosevelt's opponent (and incumbent president) Herbert Hoover, thirty-six came from the Keystone State.

Pennsylvania also bucked the majority on another key issue in '32. Nationally, even the Communist Party was more popular than the Prohibitionists. But in Pennsylvania—already closely watched and deigned by political observers for having the ability to swing the national election to one party or the other—candidates who vowed to continue the ban on alcoholic libations received twice as many votes as their Bolshevik opponents.

Only twenty-six of Pennsylvania's sixty-seven counties went for Roosevelt in 1932. One of those was Schuylkill, a county dependent on one industry: coal.

Unlike the softer bituminous coal first mined in western Pennsylvania in the 1850s, the first mine in the five-hundred-square-mile anthracite region of Pennsylvania opened in 1775, the same year the American colonies declared their intent to revolt against Great Britain. So abundant was this harder, more efficiently burning black rock that it could be seen and retrieved from outcrops along the Susquehanna River.

The earliest users of anthracite coal were confused by its properties. It did not produce flame, they complained; it just glowed. But two wire-makers working in a forge along the Schuylkill River soon came to realize that this "glow" generated tremendous heat.

In 1812, Josiah White and Erskine Hazard bought for their furnace a cartload of hard coal at a price of one dollar per bushel. After feeding the entire load into the furnace, the coal stubbornly refused to reach the temperature they needed. The men bought another cartload and spent the evening nursing what they hoped would become a roaring fire. No flames formed, and they left the furnace in disgust. One of the men—which one is no longer known—realized that he had left his coat and went back to the furnace to retrieve it. In the mere half an hour that he had been gone, the anthracite coal had transformed into a fire-red and scorching-hot solid mass. Two loads of iron were heated and rolled before the temperature finally dropped, and the two wire-makers never complained again about this marvelous power source.

In 1790, anthracite was discovered in and around what would become Schuylkill County. The Lehigh Coal Mining Company, the first commercial mining operation in the region, transported its first loads in 1820. Just two decades later, the industry experienced its first strike, which left several thousand men without work. As demand for anthracite grew, so too grew the length of miners' workdays. More time in the mines meant an escalation in miners' injury and fatality rates, and by the turn of the twentieth century, more than thirteen thousand adults and children had lost their lives as a direct or indirect result of mine accidents, explosions and fires.

By 1873, nearly the entire population of Kline Township was employed by or engaged in the coal industry. Sitting atop some of the highest elevations in the state, the Honeybrook and Silverbrook basins provided rich troves of anthracite to mine operators, who were taking almost 1,500 tons daily.

To truly understand the importance of coal to Pennsylvania's development, one needs only to consider the state hospital system and the state police. Starting in the 1870s, hospitals sprang up in the anthracite towns, their sole purpose being to treat sick and injured coal miners. In Coaldale, Schuylkill County, the Lehigh Navigation and Coal Company donated land and money to establish just such a facility. Another Schuylkill County miners' hospital, Ashland, opened in 1883. In bordering Luzerne County, the Hazleton State Hospital for Miners was established in the 1890s. Lackawanna County's Scranton State General Hospital originally opened its doors as the Lackawanna Hospital, with a mandate to treat miners in and around the city. The Shamokin State General Hospital in Northumberland County opened in 1911 to treat the miners of Coal Township. Over the years, many of these hospitals grew, added nursing programs and expanded their care giving to members of the general public. Some, like the Scranton

State General Hospital, were ultimately closed and demolished. Others, like the facilities at Coaldale and Shamokin, evolved and improved and currently operate as part of large, privately run hospital systems.

The Pennsylvania State Police can also attribute its origins to coal—but the organization is not, as many believe, an outgrowth of the Coal and Iron Police. Quite the contrary. The state police was developed to counterbalance the autonomy and lopsided enforcement activities of private officers hired by these large corporations.

In the post–Civil War era, railroads often fell victim to thieves and saboteurs, as well as to damage inflicted by hostile striking workers. In response, to protect these vital interests, in 1865, the Pennsylvania legislature granted railroads the right to hire their own protective police force. In 1866, this law was amended and broadened to include any industry with corollary interests in collieries, furnaces or rolling mills. Commissions conferring enforcement power to men selected by the rail and coal operators were available for the staggeringly low price of one dollar each. These men needed no law enforcement experience, nor was proof of fine moral, mental or physical condition a requirement for employment. The only real conditions were that badges had to read, "Coal and Iron Police," and that these "officers of the law" agreed to protect the interests of their bosses.

The first Coal and Iron Police operated in Schuylkill County and were supervised by the Pinkerton Detective Agency. This provider of private investigators and guards was a familiar presence in mining towns. Mine and railroad owners utilized Pinkerton operatives as undercover spies and union infiltrators. Pinkerton men were not above acting as "enforcers" for their employers, either. Even the federal government relied on Pinkerton's detection services when budget shortfalls precluded paying the Department of Justice to do the job. So vast did Allan Pinkerton's empire become that it was reported in the 1890s that he employed more men than the United States Army had soldiers. The sheer size and force of this body of private investigators was not lost on the coal employees the Pinkerton men patrolled.

Miners soon realized they had little power over their own choices, safety and livelihoods. Even if they gathered the strength to go on strike, it was clear that their employers, via their private militias, had the state's backing to press them back into dangerous and poorly paying jobs as quickly and ruthlessly as possible.

In 1916, Theodore Roosevelt wrote, "The labor leader who attacks the Pennsylvania State Police because it enforces the law would, if successful in the long run, merely succeed in reêntrenching in power the lawless capitalists who used the law-defying Coal and Iron Police." Roosevelt knew firsthand the need for an impartial and professional state police force, for it was during his presidency, in 1902, that the largest anthracite strike in the nation's history occurred.

Strikes were a part of the mining industry from its earliest beginnings, and with each, it seems, workers gained a bit more courage. An 1897 anthracite strike resulted in very few concessions by owners, an outcome that served only to propagate dissent. Violence erupted three years later, and two thousand national guardsmen were sent to Shenandoah, Schuylkill County, to quell the subsequent strike, in which two men were killed and seventeen wounded. After forty days of zero coal production, nearly every operator made concessions, in great part due to the efforts of a still young organization known as the United Mine Workers. In 1902, workers again sought shorter days, higher pay and full recognition of their unionized status. When operators refused, the "long strike" began.

In May 1902, nearly every employee of every mine went out on strike—even firemen and other positions. Strikers totaled nearly 150,000 persons. Again, the National Guard was called on to create and maintain peace, and this time, nearly every member of its ranks (almost 9,000 guardsmen) was required.

Negotiations between operators and miners dragged on until October; meanwhile, the cost of coal skyrocketed to the point where buyers of limited means could not afford it. Fear of a "coal famine" swept the country. With winter closing in and no agreement in sight, President Theodore Roosevelt created the Anthracite Strike Commission, which arbitrated the dispute and awarded miners most of their demands—but not before lost sales and wages neared $75 million.

In addition to its arbitration awards, the commission also took a solid position on the Coal and Iron Police. In its report, it stated: "A labor or other organization whose purpose can be accomplished only by the violation of law and order of society has no right to exist." With a finger pointed directly at Pennsylvania and its poor judgment, the commission declared that, while peace should be maintained at any cost, that cost should be borne by and made accountable to the public at large, not wealthy business owners.

By the time of the 1902 strike, public sentiment was already souring toward the monopolistic, heavy-handed mine operators and their private police force. Pennsylvanians were of a common belief that some sort of well-regulated and highly trained law enforcement body was needed to replace these men. In response, Governor Samuel W. Pennypacker signed into law Senate Act 278 on May 2, 1905. This legislation called for the formation of the Pennsylvania Mounted Police, also known as the state constabulary. The state finally had its own enforcement body under its control, not beholden to the rail and coal industries. In its first year of service, the fewer than three hundred men of the mounted police patrolled and traveled sixty-three thousand miles back and forth across the commonwealth and made 694 arrests.

For all of its good, Act 278 did not outlaw the Coal and Iron Police. Its end came in 1931, when Governor Gifford Pinchot refused to issue new, or renew old, private police commissions.

From its earliest days, Pennsylvania's state police served as a groundbreaking role model for law enforcement agencies nationwide. Companies comprising a captain, lieutenant, five sergeants and fifty offices were stationed strategically throughout the state, although initially they were most prevalent in the anthracite region. Only U.S. citizens between the ages of twenty-one and forty were eligible for appointment. They had to be literate and of good moral character and pass both physical and mental examination.

The new statewide police system changed how Pennsylvania responded to and investigated crime. Under the old sheriff and constable system, it was nearly impossible for law officers in one part of the commonwealth to know what their counterparts in other areas were doing. By contrast, state police companies operated as part of a well-informed chain of command. The concept of a main barracks from which officers could be called in an emergency, as well as the creation of small substations, is attributed to the Pennsylvania State Police. Perhaps most importantly, the assignment of a case to specific officers revolutionized the manner in which criminals were pursued and significantly increased arrests and prosecutions. Most of these ideas are attributed to the first superintendent, John C. Groome. In her 1916 book detailing the early history of the Pennsylvania State Police, Katherine Mayo describes Groome's unusually thorough approach:

> The Superintendent's first step was to make a close study of the criminal statistics of each section of the State, together with attendant conditions, in the course of which research he consulted freely with the State officials resident in the various quarters. Having clarified his conception of the actual needs of the Commonwealth by this practical procedure, he next took up the records of the various police forces of the world. He closely examined the reports of the Texas Rangers, of the Italian, the German, and the Irish forces, as well as those of the Northwestern Mounted Police of Canada, of the Australian bodies, and of others. A strict comparison of all these induced

Major Lynn G. Adams served as superintendent of the Pennsylvania State Police during the investigation into the Kelayres shootings and Joe Bruno's escape. He accompanied Schuylkill County detective Lewis Buono to New York to be part of Joe's recapture. *Image from* Smull's Legislative Hand Book and Manual of the State of Pennsylvania.

the tentative conclusion that conditions in Ireland presented a nearer parallel to the conditions in Pennsylvania than was elsewhere offered. [In Ireland] he spent three weeks in the barracks of the Royal Irish Constabulary, studying their methods, their structure, and their rules and regulations.

The morning after his return, Groome sat in the governor's office, planning the creation of Pennsylvania's first statewide police force.

At the time of the Kelayres Massacre, the superintendent of the Pennsylvania State Police was fifty-four-year-old Lynn G. Adams. Like the man who would become lieutenant governor that year, Adams hailed from the anthracite region of the state, specifically Scranton, one of its largest cities. Adams quit high school in 1898 to join the army and fight in the Spanish-American War. He continued serving in the army until 1903. In December 1905, Adams was appointed sergeant to the Pennsylvania State Police. He worked quickly up to captain, left the police force to fight in World War I and rejoined the state police upon his return home.

Superintendent Adams was a man who held law and order in high esteem. He and his men were about to cross paths with a family in Schuylkill County who did anything but.

Chapter 2

BOOTLEGGING, DRINKING AND GAMBLING

Like the sand that gradually appears along macadam roads as you drive toward the ocean, coal dust grows to slag heaps as you enter the anthracite towns of Pennsylvania. In 1936, Governor George H. Earle stated that 85 percent of the anthracite in North America was controlled by just seven companies operating in Pennsylvania. But that wasn't quite true. Hordes of miners, let go by their employers and unable to face their hungry families, turned to coal bootlegging as a means of survival and, eventually, significant profit.

A book of photographs produced about 1938 by WPA photographer Jack Delano shows in stark, sometimes troubling, detail the brutal work of mining and the hard gains of bootlegging. As if breathing coal dust and the stagnant air of the mines wasn't deadly enough, many of the miners are photographed with nonfiltered cigarettes or pipes dangling from closed lips. In the background, large stacks belch black smoke skyward. Groups of boys no more than thirteen years old survey holes from which they will remove coal that they do not own before selling it, at a good price, to men and women taking none of the risk. In one photo, a wagon full of employed miners waits to depart for Harrisburg. They are heading off to complain to the Pennsylvania legislature about the infringement of the bootleggers. One can't help but wonder if any of them hadn't, when hours were cut and money was tight, done the same thing themselves.

Bootlegging methods were as varied as the perpetrators. Some chose the "work smart, not hard" model. They stole the piles of coal unprotected

The face of a miner and an outlined portion of a Pennsylvania map showing Schuylkill County. *Image from WPA Federal Art Project Photographs of Pennsylvania Coal Miners and Coal Mining Communities.*

by, or undesirable to, the big mining operators. Others simply sank shovels into the dirt, for in many areas, coal sat so close to the surface you couldn't dig a flower garden without finding it. Still others—the bravest or most desperate—descended into closed or vacated mines, excavating by cover of night tonnage sufficient to sell. Many of these men came to be regarded as heroes. Many of their customers were friends and family members who had also lost jobs and income and for whom cheaper, bootlegged coal was

Women and girls collect coal from heaps outside closed mining offices. *Image from WPA Federal Art Project Photographs of Pennsylvania Coal Miners and Coal Mining Communities.*

a godsend. Even if they could afford "company coal," why put money in the pockets of wealthy mine operators making more money than Schuylkill County residents could even imagine?

Some coal company policies, while meant to increase owners' profits, served only to fuel the bootleggers' trade. One clear example of these poor decisions was the practice of "resizing." Anthracite coal was sold according to size and use. "Stove" coal, used for heating and cooking, was the largest and most expensive size. Coal sellers began adulterating stove coal by adding smaller pieces, coined "egg" and "pea," which burned faster, generated less heat and necessitated more reorders. Although customer complaints skyrocketed, suppliers argued that these changes were inconsequential. Regardless of the possible validity of this position, the prevailing sentiment was that coal companies were foisting less salable coal onto consumers by blending it with other grades.

Strikes also served to spur bootlegging. In addition to an interruption of miners' income, coal delivery was often embargoed while settlement talks progressed. This left whole towns with insufficient supply—a harsh prospect during biting cold winters. Bootleggers' deliveries spiked during strikes, with some enterprising suppliers traveling as far as New Jersey. Auto dealers complained that they couldn't source enough used pickup trucks to meet the demands of buyers seeking vehicles capable of hauling heavy loads. By 1935, the Bureau of Mines estimated that $20 million worth of coal had been sold illegally.

Unfortunately, the prospect of bootlegging riches lured not just experienced miners, but also many men lacking vital knowledge and experience. One bootlegger, hoping to mine an abandoned vein, found his dynamite frozen. As he tried to thaw it over the kitchen stove, the inevitable happened. Only one family member escaped death or injury. In another sad case, a thirteen-year-old boy was killed by a rockslide while aiding his father's bootlegging operation. He was buried too deeply for rescue.

But living with risk, even mortal risk, was just another day in the lives of residents of coal towns. And with the government prohibiting access to everything from coal to booze to gambling, what other choice did a hardworking man have than to find a way to supply it himself?

Recreation was an unfamiliar word in anthracite country, and entertainment was hard to come by. Gambling was the easiest and closest thing to recreation as folks could get, and the most popular vehicle for gambling during the Depression years was the slot machine. Gambling parlors operated in stealth in homes and garages, and police seemed one step behind when it came to finding and destroying this equipment. A current resident of Kelayres, Kline Township, recalls a judge who lived down the street from his father's store. Though contrary to his profession, the justice had a penchant for illegal gambling. After the judge died, the story goes, police were seen carrying slot machine after slot machine out of his home.

A bootleg miner drags on a hand-rolled cigarette. *Image from WPA Federal Art Project Photographs of Pennsylvania Coal Miners and Coal Mining Communities.*

Gambling operators were, if nothing else, ingenious. In the earliest instances of "rigging the odds," chewing gum machines were reworked to accept brass slugs the size and weight of pennies. Soon, "nickel and penny in the slot" machines were everywhere: hotels, bars, private parlors and, yes, sometimes even churches. Anti-gambling judges ordered police and sheriffs to find and destroy slots—but no sooner had one gambling parlor been raided than another appeared in its place. In once instance in 1929, $10,000 (about $136,000 in today's valuation) worth of slots was confiscated in bordering Northumberland County.

With gambling came alcohol and bootlegging of a far more famous kind. Try as they might, Prohibition Bureau police simply couldn't keep up with their mobile and financially flush prey. In 1922, state police in Pottsville executed a large and record-breaking raid. Well planned and promptly initiated to leave no time for leaks, twenty violators of the Volstead Act were arrested in one week. Based on surveillance of the movement of presumed delivery trucks, fourteen stills were confiscated in Kelayres alone. Police specifically targeted this area, having learned of the stockpiled fortunes of local (unnamed) politicians. Prior to this raid, arrests in the region were, for all intents and purposes, nonexistent.

On December 5, 1933, the Volstead Act was repealed by constitutional amendment. For Pennsylvania, this meant two things. First and foremost, it put most booze bootleggers out of business. Secondly, it created a tax bonanza for the state. In less than two years after the re-legalization of alcohol, the treasurer collected more than $12 million on the sale of malt liquor, distilled and rectified spirits and wine.

If nothing else, gambling and bootlegging proved that, even during the worst economic crash in the nation's history, there were plenty of opportunities for men and women to make money. Lots of it. And you didn't need to live in a large city to prosper. You could just as easily succeed by being a very big fish in the smallest of small ponds. That's what Joseph J. Bruno banked on. From seeding the little town of Kelayres's school board with his own supporters, to quashing Democrat opposition to his Republican machine, to reportedly bootlegging both coal and alcohol, Joe knew when to grab both financial and political reins and steer his own course. Little did "Big Joe" know that his own empire would collapse on the very same day Republicans endured the most sweeping electoral defeat in the state's history.

Chapter 3

THE BRUNO FAMILY

Honeybrook and neighboring Silverbrook, like most of Schuylkill County, were once primarily German. The agricultural sensibilities of the Deutschlanders were at odds with the coal discovered there in 1853, however, and most of these families sold their land to the mining companies. By the turn of the twentieth century, the majority of Kline Township residents were Slavic, Lithuanian, Polish and Russian, with Italians constituting a smaller, tightknit and prosperous percentage of the demography. By sheer numbers, the Italian-born Brunos were one of the most prominent families in the area. There were, in total, seven households in the township headed by Brunos—all in proximity. Several other families were related to them by marriage. Brunos were merchants, saloon owners, schoolteachers and dressmakers. But many of the first- and second-generation Brunos in America also spent time in the coal mines.

It is believed that brothers Frank, James and Peter were the first of the surname to settle in Kline Township. Frank worked his way up to mine foreman in just three years. He eventually purchased brother James's grocery shop, built a cigar factory and opened a men's shoe and apparel store in nearby McAdoo. Frank was a staunch Republican who chaired the township's party committee. He was also a school director and notary public and was appointed postmaster of Kelayres in 1899. Youngest brother Peter was also an elected official—a justice of the peace. It is Peter's name, in fact, that appears on several of the younger Brunos' marriage licenses.

When Joe and Cecelia wed, Joe gave his birth date as October 22, 1878—probably closest to his true age than other dates he provided. *From Schuylkill County marriage records.*

James Bruno arrived in America in 1879. He was twenty-five when he made the trip from Italy and was, if census records are accurate, the last of his siblings to settle in Honeybrook (later to become McAdoo and Kelayres), Kline Township, Schuylkill County. James was born in December 1854, two months before his wife, Marie.

James and Marie's first child—also their first son—was born in Italy in October 1882, according to census records. Like many details of Joseph James Bruno's life, this date of birth is perplexing since his father's arrival in the United States predates his own birth by three years. Joe's brother Philip was born in Pennsylvania in November 1885—although Marie states her year of emigration from Italy as 1886. While James could certainly have fathered Joe on a visit home to Italy, there is no explanation for son Phil, who was purportedly birthed in Pennsylvania a year before his mother arrived here.

Regardless of which source you use, a definitive birth date for Joe is hard to come by. Joe married fifteen-year-old Cecelia Rizzuto on October 26, 1900. The marriage license gives his birth date as October 22, 1878, making Joe—who named as his profession "bartender"—twenty-two years old. In 1918, when he registered as part of the World War I draft, Joe gives his birth date as October 21, 1882, which matches census records. A World War II draft registration offers a date of birth of October 21, 1884. Joe's death certificate gives one final—and completely different—date of birth: October 20, 1888.

Whatever the truth of his age might be, Joe named his own firstborn son after his father. Baby James was born about 1903, but like Joe's and Cecelia's, this date fluctuated over the years. Next came daughter Antoinette, as fiercely loyal to Joe as any male scion could be. Later came Alfred, Elveda and Ernest.

All of the Brunos attended the Church of the Immaculate Conception, located directly across the street from Joe's house. Founded in 1899, the parish had charge of all Italians in Kelayres, McAdoo, Treskow, Jeansville and Holly. Joe's second-floor bedroom windows looked down over the church and onto the intersection of Fourth and Centre Streets. These same windows also offered an obstructed view of the building catty-corner to Joe's house. This building was owned by John Salidago, and Joe's nephew Paul rented an apartment on the second floor. Like Joe, Paul had a clear view of the familiar corner.

Also close to Joe's home sat a small, wooden schoolhouse. It served all of the children of the village of Kelayres. Divided into grades just a few years earlier, by 1893, the growth of the town had necessitated a one-room addition. State-run Normal School graduates filled most of the teaching positions in Pennsylvania by the start of the twentieth century, but in some areas—like Kline Township—teachers were still appointed by school boards. Control of the Kelayres School administrators and teachers was of primary importance to Joe Bruno, as was the school itself. Not long before the election of 1934, he had the wooden structure torn down and replaced it with a new, two-story brick building. The Bruno School was just one more slow-burning fuse leading directly to the Kelayres Massacre.

Chapter 4

SEEDS OF A REVOLT

Kelayres was never what one might describe as a sleepy small town. Between the racket of the breakers and coal shoots, the rumble of wagons and trucks and the dynamiting of stubborn coal veins, peace was hard to find. It took a special kind of man—or woman—to settle in Kelayres. A rugged and brave sort. Life in the village wasn't suited to the meek.

It was not unusual to hear of Kelayres blast setters accidentally destroying a family's home in their attempts to find coal. And it was commonplace to hear of arguments (often fueled by alcohol) escalating to physical confrontations or even shootings. No story better illustrates this peculiar cycle than a 1915 incident in which a Kelayres schoolteacher by the name of Elizabeth Cara resigned her position to marry James Palura, whom her father had recently shot through the lung. Fortunately for Mr. Cara, his jail sentence was suspended when doctors determined that Palura would likely survive.

While some slights were contested, resolved and forgotten, others festered like infected wounds. Such was the case in the battle for control of the Kelayres School. School directors were elected to their positions. Schoolteachers were selected by directors. The choice of school directors therefore made all the difference, and teachers (and parents) felt the pressure of making the "right" choice in the voting booth. While the nation in 1934 may have been asking itself if it wanted a New Deal, for the people of Kelayres, the question was much simpler: did they want McAlooses or Brunos running the school?

It was in 1907 that Joe Bruno, his brother Philip and their cousin Louis first accepted the reins of leadership from their elders. In that year, in

Above: This kitchen is typical of that found in the homes of anthracite miners' families. *Image from WPA Federal Art Project Photographs of Pennsylvania Coal Miners and Coal Mining Communities.*

Left: Portrait of Joe Bruno, clearly showing his signature gold pocket chain and elk tooth charm. *Image courtesy of Deborah Motika.*

what many in Kelayres considered a questionable election, Joe became school board director, Louis took the job as school principal and Philip became a tax collector. There is little question that these three men believed they would, in turn, pass down the town to their own children—an inheritance to which the three Bruno men thought their offspring were simply entitled.

Throughout the years leading up to the massacre, Joe's influence and positions of importance grew. He would become an assistant county detective, run for and win the office of justice of the peace, assume a director position at the bank, garage and maintain the school buses (for which he charged a healthy fee) and even sell the gasoline on which the buses ran. When a house became available in Kelayres, Joe Bruno often installed family members—many of whom left Italy to share in the family's American fortunes. As both a bank director and landlord, however, Joe had power over other homeowners and tenants as well.

Joe's detractors were less than charitable in their characterizations. He was regarded as nothing more than a bootlegger, slot runner, election rigger and loan shark. He strong-armed competitors, they said, using physical violence if necessary. He tampered with juries and mortgaged homes in exchange for pledges of loyalty—and foreclosed on those who dared challenge him. He was accused of expecting "favors" from the young, female teachers he personally interviewed and hired.

Not surprisingly, those closest to Joe held—and some still hold—far more favorable opinions. A living descendant says that the reason for the town's bitterness toward Joe can be attributed to one age-old motivation: envy. He was a successful man with the kind of money and power less fortunate coal town residents coveted. "He did run the town. He was very wealthy," says granddaughter Deborah Bruno Motika, who was born after Joe's death. She describes herself as the family historian—and the only one who still has an active interest in preserving Joe's legacy. As for the accusations of election fraud, Motika is matter-of-fact in her assessment: "That has always gone on in Kelayres. We had a vote rigging [scandal] just twenty years ago."

Motika is equally forthcoming about Joe's sources of revenue. According to family lore passed down to her, Joe traveled to Pottsville every Sunday morning to collect money from the bordello he operated there. His daughter Elveda sometimes went along for the ride. While she waited outside in the car, the working girls would bring her candy. Motika also remembers the pool hall next to Joe's home that did double duty as the Republican headquarters. "It was still a pool hall when I was a child," she says.

As for the arsenal of weapons stored in the Bruno bedroom and elsewhere throughout the home, Motika offers an easy explanation: "They believed in protecting themselves." And, she explains, Joe and his sons were avid hunters and gun collectors. "Many of those weapons came from Europe and were collectors' items."

Without question, Joe Bruno had more to protect than many of his neighbors. In a time when Sears Kenmore clothes washers cost $44.95 and tires were $3.60 a piece, the Bruno home built in 1927 was reportedly worth $25,000.00 (about $350,000.00 today), four times that of the other houses on his block. It was, in fact, twice as valuable as the second most expensive home in the township. And rightfully so. Its solid brick exterior sheaths twelve-inch plaster-coated walls. The trim, floors and interior doors are solid oak. Leaded glass panes fill the three sets of double doors, creating the private sitting room in the front of the house. A fireplace fills the wall of the family room that spills into the dining room. "It's like a fortress," says current owner Lucille Trella. She purchased the home from Elveda Bruno, Joe's daughter, the last family member to live there. Lucille's mother did not march in the parade on the night of November 5, 1934, but she stood along the street as it passed and spoke often of the massacre. Lucille has her own personal recollections of the Brunos. "They were nice people," she says, outside of their suspect activities.

But by the 1920s, another family of strong political mindset was building influence in Kline Township—a family that believed Joe's nice veneer hid a common and ugly ambition.

Chapter 5

THE MCALOOSE FACTION

Although it sounds Anglicized, the McAloose family was every bit as Italian as the Brunos. The spelling "Macaluso" (found in both historical and contemporary Schuylkill County records) is probably closest to how the surname was crafted in its native country, but the number of spelling variations sprinkled throughout public records makes a definitive determination impossible.

There were five families headed by McAlooses at the time of the massacre, four of whom resided within Kelayres. The fifth, headed by the widow Magdeline McAloose, lived in neighboring McAdoo Heights. The McAloose clan was not without means. Dan McAloose's house in Kelayres was valued at $6,000 in 1930. Magdeline's home was valued at $10,000—not Bruno money but an astronomical amount for that time and place. Magdeline had four sons. John, born in Italy, was the eldest. Next came Joseph and then Carl, born in 1902. Louis, born stateside, was the youngest. John, Carl and Dan McAloose were all publicly vocal in their anti-Bruno beliefs and support for unionizing schoolteachers. They believed this change, like cleaving the proverbial snakehead from its body, would effectively neutralize the nepotism and favoritism embedded in the current hiring system. After all, if a schoolteacher could rely on tenure or collective bargaining to ensure job security, there would be no reason to pander to (or fear) the Brunos.

The feud between the Bruno-ites and the McAloose faction had been brewing for years. It nearly came to a violent end in 1933, when the election ballot included school directors, tax collector, justice of the peace, judge of election and other local offices. Both sides campaigned heavily, and opposing ads appeared side by side in local newspapers. Bruno's team took the tried-and-true Republican approach: a vote for Kline Township Democrats is a vote for higher taxes. Dems touted the fact that former Socialist Joseph L. Gallagher had withdrawn his candidacy under that party and thrown his hat to the Blue Eagle and Democrat candidate. Come election day, turnout was high on both sides.

When the votes were counted, it appeared that it was the McAloose-supported Democrats who had prevailed. As justice of the peace, however, Joe Bruno seized the ballot box and took it home, where it was kept for several days before he delivered it to county officials for a recount. During the recount, some citizens complained of visible erasure marks and after-the-fact changes. Seven hundred residents went before election judge G. Harold Watkins to re-record their true voting intent. This evidence seemed to support the Democrats' claims of victory, yet Watkins declared Bruno and his Republicans the winners. Enraged, opponents took the election to court, but the case was not called quickly enough for frustrated townspeople.

In August 1934, as children tried to return to school after summer break, hostilities between Republicans and Democrats reached dangerous and irrational heights. Both parties shouted and argued about their self-proclaimed election wins. Republicans hurriedly named their own staff of teachers and opened the school for registration. Democrats, unable to counter quickly enough with their own teacher appointments, instead tried to wrest away control of the school buses. Rowdies on both sides threw stones and brawled. One teacher, Anna McDonald, suffered a broken arm as she tried to board one of the buses for shelter. The state police was finally called to end the fighting, and principal William Minor closed the schools until the damage could be repaired.

In retrospect, one can't help but wonder what would have happened if the 1933 election had been fairly contested and the Democrats immediately named the winners. Would the massacre of the following year still have happened? Or would it only have come sooner?

Chapter 6

A PARADE ENDS
IN BLOODSHED

November 5, 1934, was election eve in every one of the forty-eight states in the nation except Maine, the residents of which had voted in September. Polling indicated that the Democrats enjoyed a consistent national lead running up to the election, so pundits focused more on state-level elections—particularly those in Pennsylvania and Nebraska, where it was all about the New Deal or no deal.

The race in Pennsylvania was expected to be tight. Everyone—Republicans, Democrats, newspapers, community groups, churches—urged voters to get out and do their civic duty. The state's voter registration topped four million names, more than at any previous time. Three-quarters of those registered voters were expected to turn out. Although overall percentages favored the Republicans, trending seemed to favor the Democrats, whose registration had increased over the previous two years, while their opponents' had declined.

Only half of the state's precincts would vote using machines. Nearly four thousand polling places were still using paper ballots. Newspapers touted their offices as the only source for up-to-the-minute election results, but it depended on where they were located when it came to estimating wait times. In Delaware County, the *Chester Times* told readers it would broadcast election results from its offices by loudspeaker. That paper predicted that, since the Philadelphia metro area it served would primarily vote by machine, results would be available early. The more rural *Indiana Evening Gazette* also invited the public to visit or call its offices to learn election results, but its editors warned that these calls should not be made until after nine o'clock on election night since "tallying of votes will be a long, tedious affair."

Pennsylvania's Democratic candidates not only supported FDR but also ran almost exclusively on Roosevelt's policies and coattails. Republicans responded with a call to vote for "a square deal, not a New Deal" and believed the commonwealth's voters would soundly reject the president's excessive spending. The cost of his programs was indeed staggering. In less than two years, expenditures neared $11 billion (about $18 million per day), and FDR was prepared to spend an additional $5 billion. The money funded new programs such as Social Security—a plan opponents considered akin to socialism. It also covered the costs of stimulus programs such as the Civilian Conservation Corps and the Public Works Administration.

Pennsylvania Republican Party spokesman M. Harvey Taylor predicted that every one of his candidates on the state ticket would be propelled to victory.

In Kelayres, the evening of November 5, 1934, was cool and dark. The sun fully set just before five o'clock. The waning moon barely offered light. Emboldened by the strides the party was making nationally, and by their belief that they had indeed won the 1933 local elections, the Democrats of Kline Township felt good about their chances. This, they believed, was the year that Joe Bruno's reign as Republican boss would end.

Both parties held election eve rallies. The Dems met in McAdoo, where the McAloose headquarters was situated. The Republicans met in Joe's pool hall cum party headquarters. If Joe sensed defeat, he didn't show it publicly. But behind the scenes, there were rumblings about his growing anger. Some said he'd been making threats toward the Democrats. Privately, he *must* have doubted whether his machine could withstand another close—or stolen—election.

By evening, the Democrats' confidence that they might just pull it off this time had graduated to a feeling of inevitability. The majority of the townspeople seemed to support them. If everyone who said they backed the Democrats actually voted, Bruno and his family and cronies would be history. The McAloose faction knew it had to keep the momentum going if it was to succeed in getting enough people to the polls to win the election.

At about nine o'clock that evening, someone suggested a parade. Democrats and Bruno opponents turned out by the dozens in the well-dressed style befitting the 1930s. Most of the men wore felt hats and knee-length wool dress coats over properly starched shirts with ties. The women were equally fashionable, most with perfectly coiffed hair, nylon-sheathed legs and shoes normally reserved for the finest occasions.

Though hastily planned, a few basic decisions were made. Youngsters would ride in the back of an open truck near the head of the parade. Men, women and older children would march. A standard-bearer would lead the parade carrying an American flag. Lanterns would light the way when streetlights did not. But somewhere during the march, another decision was made. They would pass by the Bruno home—to taunt the Republican boss and his family about what would surely be their final fall from grace, a loss dealt by the hands of their own neighbors.

No one disagrees that the Democrats purposefully approached the Bruno home. Very few argue about what happened when they did. Only the Brunos debated the source of—and reason for—the gunfire.

The intersection of Centre and Fourth Streets is small. To stand in it and imagine being fired on is horrifying. There is no place to hide. Running only served to make the victims moving—yet still clearly visible—targets.

The Immaculate Conception Roman Catholic Church sits on the southeast corner of the intersection. Directly across the street on the southwest corner was Joe Bruno's home. The home of James Bruno, Joe's son, sat next to his father's. Diagonally from Joe, on the northeast corner, is the brick home and former drugstore then (and now) owned by the Salidago family, who had recently switched alliances. After years of standing with the Brunos, in 1934, they supported the Democrats' plan to ouster the clan. Yet on the second floor, above the little store that sold two-cent ice cream cones, Paul Bruno—Joe's nephew—rented an apartment.

Immediately neighboring the Salidagos was Frank Fiorella, a dapper man in his mid-sixties, recognizable by his full silver hair and mustache. Frank's daughter Jennie had married Joe Bruno's archrival Dan McAloose.

Frank Fiorella was born in Italy in April 1863. He immigrated to the United States in 1888, but not before marrying. By 1900, he was living in Kelayres, working as a day laborer in the mines. He couldn't read or write English, but he could speak it. His first house was a rental. Over the next twenty years, he continued to work in the mines, eventually earning enough money to buy his own home, a portion of which he rented out. Fiorella's sons followed in their father's footsteps, working as miners, brakemen, firemen and coal strippers.

On the night of November 5, Fiorella's son-in-law stopped by to talk about the election. No doubt, Fiorella and McAloose also spoke of the parade that would pass close to Fiorella's front door and serve as one final rallying cry for victory at the polls.

One of the last gatherings of Democrats prior to the parade occurred on the front porch of Nicholas Perna's home. Perna lived, as did Joe Bruno, on Centre Street. Eleven short blocks in length, Centre Street was home to several additional key players in the ongoing feud, including John McAloose, other Fiorella and Forke family members and Joe Bruno's brother Phil. The tightknit placement of such bitterly embattled men and women makes it unbelievable that violence had not erupted earlier and more often.

People of the village lined the streets to see the parade, many of them young girls whose parents would not let them march. Parade walkers' lanterns cast just enough light to see the road a few steps ahead. The procession headed up Centre Street, which, at the lighted intersection with Fourth, ran alongside Joe Bruno's property. Straight ahead of them on the left was the Salidagos' store and on the right, the Immaculate Conception Church. Twenty-one-year-old Carl Vacante, carrying the American flag, made a right turn. This would take the marchers directly in front of the Bruno home, from which the parade could now be viewed from both the side and front second-story bedroom windows.

According to thirteen-year-old James Dolan, the Brunos were spoiling for a fight from the beginning. About an hour before the parade started, Antoinette Billig and several others had climbed into a big Nash, said Dolan, and sped toward the Democrats' headquarters. He and a few other children ran after the car, yelling, "Hurrah for the Democrats!" When the car stopped and one of its occupants fired three shots over their heads, the children thought better of their taunting and remained in place near the Bruno home. When the car returned, Dolan and his friends watched as Joe's son Alfred and three other women gathered stones from the driveway before heading into the Bruno garage.

Mrs. Charles Grego, who was in attendance at a meeting inside the Democrat headquarters, said she, too, heard the shots from the passing Bruno cars, supporting the boy's account.

There are varying versions of how and when the shooting actually started. Some said the shots fired over the heads of the children were a signal to the Brunos that the parade was forming. Other witnesses said that it was Tony Orlando who first fired a pistol into the crowd while standing on the front lawn of Joe Bruno's home. Other accounts place a shooter on Centre Street between the Salidago drugstore and the Immaculate Conception Church, firing on the marchers as they turned to go past Joe Bruno's house. Still others say it was James Bruno, who lived next door to his father, Joe, who fired the first shots from his own front yard while shouting, "What the hell are you people doing here?"

However it began, so many shots were fired in such rapid succession that the first callers to the police substation in Tamaqua reported machine gun fire in the tiny town of Kelayres, an erroneous conclusion that a number of newspapers reported as well. Officers answering the phone assumed there must be some mistake, as callers said the gunshots were coming from the home of county detective Joe Bruno. These people were either confused or pulling a prank, they decided. Why would a detective open fire on his own unarmed townspeople? Meanwhile, the shooting continued.

Stanley Kordish and Adolph Payer were marching side by side. As they approached the Bruno home, Payer noticed that all of the windows were closed. A moment later, shots rang out. After fleeing for cover, Payer noticed that Bruno's side bedroom window now stood halfway open. Shortly afterward, the two men heard shots coming from the front of the house.

Joseph DeMario didn't see or hear shots coming from the side window but heard at least a dozen blasts of gunfire come from the front upstairs

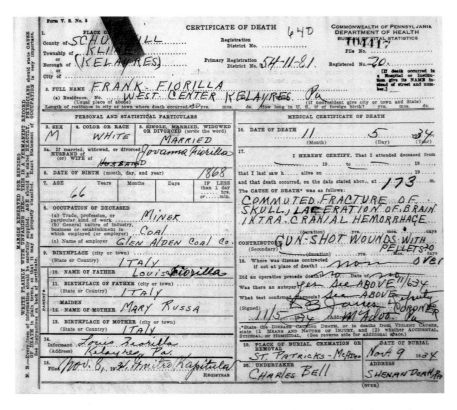

Frank Fiorella was the first to die as he stood in front of his home watching the parade. A direct blast to the head killed him outright. Young, athletic John Galosky ran to his aid, not knowing Fiorella was already dead. Galosky, too, was shot and killed. *From Pennsylvania Department of Health death certificates.*

Space for additional information by physician

THIS MAN WAS STANDING ON. THE STREET OF KELAYRES Pa WATCHING A. DEMOCRATIC PARADE WAS. SHOT. FROM The HOME OF Mr. J.J. BRUNO HIT BY PELLETS DIED OUT. RIGHT.

As evidenced by the back of Fiorella's death certificate, there is no question about the coroner's opinion on the cause of death. *From Pennsylvania Department of Health death certificates.*

windows. In separate statements, Rose Dino, Jennie Dino and Joseph Cara described the exact same thing.

The first man to fall was Frank Fiorella. He was standing on the northwest corner of the intersection in front of what was then the Marko building, a butcher shop with second-floor apartments. The twenty-gauge rifle pellets fractured his skull and pierced his brain. The resulting intra-cranial hemorrhage killed him outright.

Young, fit football player John Galosky rushed toward Fiorella, hoping to protect him from further injury, not realizing the man was already beyond help. Another volley of blasts broke out, and Galosky, too, fell. Dozens of shots ripped into his back, spun him around and then tore through his midsection.

Both Dominic Perna and Andrew Kostishion were also felled by body shots. Perna, who unwittingly made himself an easy target by standing under a streetlight, suffered shotgun wounds to the chest and abdomen. He died before help could arrive, although there was little chance of his survival under the best of circumstances. Kostishion was not part of the parade but rather ran to the intersection when he heard gunfire, for he knew his daughter was somewhere in the crowd. The shots to his abdomen lacerated his spleen. He lingered into the next day before succumbing to his injuries.

Several people took refuge under the porch steps of the Immaculate Conception Church. Mildred Vendura ran there to hide herself and her young daughter. William Forke, whose wide grin beams out of a photo taken not long before the massacre, also took cover under the wooden structure alongside Mary Dvorak. During a lull, and believing the shooting to be over, Forke left his hiding place to check on the condition of his injured neighbors. A gunshot rang out. The bullet found its mark and lacerated Forke's liver, stomach, small intestine and kidney, leaving massive internal trauma. His death would have been painful and likely not as quick as would have been humane. Ironically, it was Forke—who suffered the most extensive physical punishment—whose case would be tried last.

The once jubilant parade now descended into utter chaos. Shots seemed to come from everywhere. No one was spared; even two teenage girls fleeing

Mary Dvorak heard the gunshots and tried to run. A bullet entered the right side of her right shoe, passed through her nylon stocking and foot and then exited the other side of the shoe. *Photograph taken by author at Pennsylvania State Police Historical, Educational and Memorial Center.*

for the safety of the McAloose home were shot in the legs as they ascended the stairs. Several other women, including schoolteacher Irene Condor and Frank Fiorella's daughter, were shot in the legs or hips or both. Edward Vespucci was shot in the head. He survived, but the bullet remained there for the rest of his life. John Salidago, owner of the apartment building in which Paul Bruno lived, was shot and hospitalized, his prognosis grim.

An injury dramatically illustrated by surviving evidence is the wound to the foot of Mary Dvorak, who, like Forke, mistakenly thought she could run from the gunmen. A bullet entered the right side of her right foot. It passed through the blue leather tie-up dress shoe, then her nylon stocking and completely through her flesh and bones before exiting the stocking and shoe's opposite side. Both the footwear and stocking were collected as evidence and presented at trial. These items today are housed and preserved by the Pennsylvania State Police Historical, Educational and Memorial Center.

Investigators calculated that twenty-six people were injured in the shooting, although it must have been a daunting task to discern the wounded from the

A blood-soaked tie found at the scene. The evidence tag has been lost, but it is believed it was worn by one of the murder victims. In the 1970s, it was one of the exhibits in a display case at the Pennsylvania State Police headquarters in Hershey. *Photograph taken by author at Pennsylvania State Police Historical, Educational and Memorial Center.*

Like the blood-soaked tie, this felt hat still bears witness to the injuries of its wearer. Pellet holes from the assailant are clearly visible. It is very similar to a hat worn by William Forke taken shortly before the massacre. *Photograph taken by author at Pennsylvania State Police Historical, Educational and Memorial Center.*

bystanders, many of whom were unharmed but splashed with the blood of fellow parade marchers. Even the American flag lay on the ground, dotted with tiny holes left by the deadly shotgun pellets. Nothing was spared from the hail of gunfire, not brick, sidewalks or windows. The carnage inflicted on human targets was, of course, the most savage, and coroner John Daily reported that, during postmortem examinations, he had removed both rifle bullets and hundreds of shotgun pellets from the bodies of the dead. He also found evidence of what are known, in police parlance, as "through and throughs"—bullets that entered and exited the body, leaving only a gaping hole behind.

By the time the first police arrived, the firing and chaos had died away, and the only sounds were the moans of the wounded and the wailing of the dead's survivors. But as shock and confusion faded, anger grew, and soon there rose a more organized cry: the call to dynamite the Bruno home.

Although hard pressed to maintain it at times, police formed a protective ring around the Brunos' brick fortress. Officers entering the home were shocked at the arsenal in the upstairs bedroom. There they found three rifles, three shotguns and six revolvers. Loaded ammunition included ninety-six twelve-gauge shells, 218 .32-caliber bullets, 100 .25-caliber bullets and 75 .351-caliber bullets. Even the drawer of the downstairs sewing machine held a bullet. Nineteen spent shotgun cartridges littered the bedroom. More weapons and ammunition, including an unloaded twelve-gauge Winchester pump rifle, were found in the apartment of Paul Bruno. As the investigation progressed, the inventory of Joe's arsenal grew to include thirteen sticks of dynamite, more shells and additional firearms.

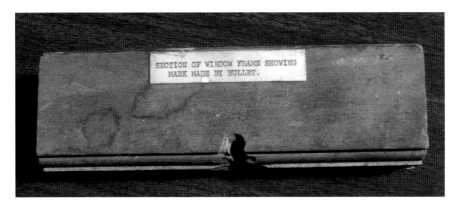

A section of window frame (possibly from the home of Dan McAloose) showing a bullet hole.
Photograph taken by author at Pennsylvania State Police Historical, Educational and Memorial Center.

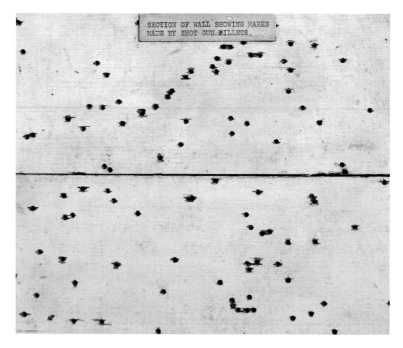

A section of the wall of an unidentified home riddled with pellet holes during the Kelayres Massacre. *Photograph taken by author at Pennsylvania State Police Historical, Educational and Memorial Center.*

This police photo, taken the morning after the massacre, perfectly illustrates the gloom hanging over the tiny town of Kelayres on election day in 1934. *From Schuylkill County Historical Society.*

Sometime after midnight, when election eve officially passed into election day, the rain started. By the relative safety of the light of dawn, Joe Bruno and the other occupants of his home were—under armed protection—ushered into waiting police cars and taken to the Tamaqua substation for questioning before being driven to the Schuylkill County Prison. Those arrested were Joe; his wife, Cecelia; their daughter Elveda; Joe's sons Alfred and James; his sister Lucy Bruno; his nephew Paul Bruno; Joe's brother Phil; Phil's son Arthur; a bus driver named Peter Russo; and three Bruno-appointed schoolteachers, Julia Lesko, Eva Socker and Cecelia Straka.

There was no sunlight when the rest of the town woke, but the sky was sufficiently bright for residents of Kelayres to see the puddles of mud and blood standing in their streets. The lust for revenge was palpable, but not the kind the Bruno clan had dispensed. The retaliation Kelayres sought was the kind that would hurt Joe Bruno far more than bullets ever could.

Chapter 7

THE ELECTION OF 1934

As Pennsylvanians finished their dinners on the evening of November 6, 1934, they opened their late-edition newspapers to headlines that, though varying in composition, all suggested the same thing: an unprecedented number of the state's registered voters (nearly 96 percent) had turned out to vote in that day's election. In slightly smaller type, but sharing the front page, was another story describing a shooting in a little town in Schuylkill County that had left three dead and two at death's door.

Contrary to the predictions of political pundits, persistent rainfall and dropping temperatures did not deter Keystone State voters, many of whom—to the surprise of poll workers—waited in line even before precinct doors were unlocked.

By November 7, the story of the "Kelayres Massacre" was every bit as large as the Democrats' landslide in Pennsylvania, and the nation was immediately transfixed by the event.

In the space of a few hours, Kelayres transformed from an obscure mining town few had heard of and even fewer visited to front-page news in papers from Winnipeg to San Antonio to San Francisco.

The rest of the nation assumed the shootings were politically motivated, but this big picture view was, in reality, far too wide. Still, Democrats grabbed on to this convenient storyline with both hands, and the state's party headquarters issued the following statement:

At this moment four are dead [the original, erroneous tally], *six are reported dying and several others, including a school teacher, are wounded. They were shot down in cold blood and their blood is on the hands of the Republican party as it goes to the polls.*

Republican gang leaders are playing their last card. Information is that one man has [also] *been murdered in Philadelphia, and that gangs of gunmen have been patrolling the streets of Philadelphia.*

The Republican campaign of terrorism is an attempt to end government by ballot—and to substitute government by machine guns.

Democrat-leaning newspaper editors were equally vociferous in their judgment. "The assassins who fired into a Democratic political parade," wrote the editor of the *Pittsburg Press*, "should not be allowed to 'get away' with [it]… or the public inevitably will suspect that county and state officials—most of whom are Republicans—have 'pulled their punches' because of politics."

Meanwhile, some Republicans decried the event as ethnically, rather than politically, motivated—a case of Italian immigrants against Eastern European immigrants. In his statement, Republican Party state chair M. Harvey Taylor wholeheartedly defended his party:

All good citizens will deplore such disorders as are reported from Schuylkill County, and all good citizens will heartily approve the prompt announcement of William A. Schnader that as attorney general he will send, if necessary, special prosecutors to see that justice is done.

So far as I can learn from reading newspapers, there was more of a personal animosity than there was a political factionalism in the outbreak. But whatever the cause, that sort of thing is abhorrent to all decent people.

The Republican party stands for clean, orderly elections, its representatives in the state government are to be commended for the prompitude [sic] *of their action and it is to be hoped that an example will be made of those responsible, so that there shall be no more such disgraceful occurrences in this state.*

Outgoing governor Gifford Pinchot was most accurate about the true nature of the massacre, very likely because he was getting information from state police superintendent Lynn G. Adams, a native of the anthracite region:

Major Adams of the state police with which I got in touch at once informs me that these killings are the outcome of a long-standing local quarrel. His men have already made several arrests and are searching for the machine guns [another early and erroneous report] *which are supposed to have been used in the killings.*

Regardless of the actual facts, the Kelayres Massacre blended, in many minds, with the surging popularity of the Democrats and growing distrust of Republicans, whom it seemed would deter opposition by any means necessary. Though the shooting had little if any bearing on statewide voting results, the election was a resounding success for Pennsylvania's Democrats. This, in turn, cemented for Roosevelt an unimpeachable mandate. No longer could Republicans threaten to overturn the president's social programs. The New Deal was a done deal, and it was here to stay.

By anyone's measure, the election was everything FDR could have dreamed of and more. Although 1934 was an off-year election (no presidential race), an unprecedented and record-setting number of voters went to the polls to hand the Democrats—in addition to countless state offices—a two-thirds majority in the United States Senate. But nowhere were the results more dramatic than in Pennsylvania, where, for the first time in more than four decades, a Democrat was elected to the office of governor. For the first time in sixty years, Pennsylvanians elected a Democrat to the U.S. Senate. And for the first time since the Civil War, Democrats controlled the state House. Even with its seemingly insurmountable advantage of one and a quarter million more registered voters, Pennsylvania Republicans could not impede what was so crushing a Democratic tide that it swept all statewide candidates into office. M. Harvey Taylor's prediction of a complete party sweep was on the money; he just called it for the wrong party.

In tiny Kelayres, the voting tallies were equally, if not more, stunning. The Associated Press reported that, of 686 votes cast, only 24 went to Bruno's Republican candidates. It was a devastating defeat for a man who came to expect and enjoy 89 percent of the small town's support.

Almost one full month after the shooting, another political blow befell Big Joe: the Schuylkill County court decided, once and for all, that Bruno opponents had indeed won that fiercely contested 1933 Kline Township election. This meant that Joe's teachers were out. More embarrassing, he was out as school director. Son James's position at the First National Bank in McAdoo was terminated, and Joe was asked to resign from that bank's board.

It seemed that even before his trial had begun, the people of Kline Township passed judgment against the despoiled Republican leader. Regardless of what his jury might decide, Joe Bruno received from his fellow townspeople a life sentence: he would never regain his political or personal capital, nor would his home ever again be the sole seat of power in Kelayres. In trying to bend one little village to his will, Bruno gave the people and party he despised more collective momentum than he ever imagined they might possess. And they were using it against him.

Chapter 8

THE FUNERALS

Just days after their historic victories, Pennsylvania's newly elected and highest-ranking officials served as honorary pallbearers for the five men murdered in the Kelayres Massacre. A town that received little if any attention from politicians outside of the community found itself host to United States senator-elect Joseph F. Guffy, Governor-elect George H. Earle and both the incoming lieutenant governor and secretary of internal affairs. Attorney General–elect Charles J. Margiotti traveled separately and joined the others in Kline Township. Prior to the burials, these officeholders visited with the families of the dead, a show of respect that enjoyed great coverage by the press.

Governor Earle carried his hat in his hand as he walked with the hearses, a respectful gesture in keeping with the somber event. In truth, however, Earle could not have been more different than the families he consoled. Born to a wealthy Chester County family, Earle attended both the blue-blooded Delancey School in Philadelphia and Harvard University. Like most wealthy scions, he completed his preparations for the professional world with a stay abroad. Upon returning to Pennsylvania, he joined his father in the sugar industry.

In 1916, following an attack by revolutionary Pancho Villa on an American town in New Mexico, Earle enlisted in the Second Pennsylvania Infantry. He served on the Mexican border under General John J. Pershing and earned a second lieutenant's commission. When the United States entered the First World War, Earle once again enlisted. He earned the Navy

Governor George H. Earle would become the first Democrat elected to the office of governor in four decades but would serve only one term. *Image from* Smull's Legislative Hand Book and Manual of the State of Pennsylvania.

Cross by leading his men off the USS *Victor*, a wooden-hulled boat nearly decimated by an explosion in its engine room.

In 1932, Earle was appointed minister plenipotentiary to the Republic of Austria. It was a turbulent time for that nation and, indeed, the rest of the world. Adolf Hitler and Nazism were growing in power and appetite, and Earle was outspoken about his belief in the threat of both. It was from this ministerial position that Earle resigned to take up his candidacy for Pennsylvania governor. Little did he know that before he could even take the oath of office, he would find himself leading the funeral procession of five murder victims in a little anthracite town in Schuylkill County.

Unlike George H. Earle, Lieutenant Governor Thomas Kennedy possessed an intimate knowledge of the lives the people of Schuylkill County led. Born in neighboring Carbon County and educated only in public schools, he entered the coal mines in his

Lieutenant Governor Thomas Kennedy, a native of Pennsylvania's anthracite region, also served as an officer of the United Mine Workers of America. *Image from* Smull's Legislative Hand Book and Manual of the State of Pennsylvania.

youth and remained in the industry throughout his life. At the time of the election, he served as secretary treasurer of the United Mine Workers of America.

The victims' survivors may have appreciated and even enjoyed the presence of such powerful men, but they were nonetheless devastated and angry at their losses. Frank Fiorella left behind five full-grown children and a sixty-five-year-old wife. Dominic Perna's survivors included his parents, siblings and twenty-eight-year-old widow. Andrew Kostishion's three young daughters would now be cared for by his wife, Anna, with the help of his parents, who lived next door. William Forke's three children, including a son who was the spitting image of his dad, would likewise be raised fatherless. On daughter Theresa's 1945 marriage license, the line for the name of her father contained only the word "deceased."

Last rites for Fiorella, Perna and Forke were held at the Church of the Immaculate Conception, in keeping with their Italian heritage. Kostishion

A police photo showing the scene on Centre Street, taken from Joe's second-story bedroom window. The Immaculate Conception Roman Catholic Church, where several of the murder victims' funerals were held, faces Joe's front door. *From Schuylkill County Historical Society.*

and Galosky's funerals were held at a church in nearby Lofty. Afterward, all five coffins were transported to their respective cemeteries.

The funeral procession was an awesome spectacle—a unique knitting of ethnicity, mourning and photo opportunities. *Time* magazine sent a reporter to cover the final tributes to these previously unknown men, as did the *New York Times* and countless other newspapers. An estimated ten thousand onlookers lined the streets as the processional passed, and a postcard later sold in the Salidago drugstore seems to support this number. In the black-and-white photo, five large hearses driving side by side lead a motorcade through McAdoo, while men and women, wedged shoulder to shoulder, watched from the sidewalks. The closure of the mines, stores and businesses helped swell attendance.

It is said that a group of crying Italian women approached Governor Earle, shouting an animated appeal in their native tongue, a message translated by Margiotti, who, though born in Punxatawney, was the son of Italian-speaking parents. "See that these murderers are killed," the women swore, "because if the law doesn't, we will do it ourselves."

Chapter 9

PRISONER JOSEPH J. BRUNO

In 1910, the Schuylkill County Prison was described in a newspaper article as the most secure prison in the state of Pennsylvania, second only to the notorious Eastern State Penitentiary in Philadelphia. Ironically, however, this statement was made in an article discussing the recent escape of two prisoners for whom authorities still searched.

Like many prisons of its era, Pottsville's jail was built to frighten. A sinister version of the castles populating children's fairy tales, the prison sits atop its apex and looks down over the town's residents just as a harsh schoolteacher might look down at her small pupils. Don't make a mistake, it seems to say, or you'll have to deal with me.

As is the case with most institutions in Pennsylvania's anthracite region, the Schuylkill County Prison has its own unbreakable connection to coal. In 1877, six of the ten convicted Mollie Maguires—Irish coal labor organizers—were hanged in the prison yard. Executions were public spectacles then, and sometimes as many as five hundred morbidly curious townspeople crowded through the prison gates to watch the hangings. Other prisoners chose to take their own lives rather than face whatever the courts might serve them, so the prison annals are also replete with sad tales of suicide.

Prisoner Joseph J. Bruno was not worried about life inside, for there was very little difference between his days at home and those confined. The truth is that Schuylkill County's jail was Joe's final fiefdom—his last seat of power. Had he served his full sentence there, prison life would have been a cakewalk.

The Schuylkill County Prison—or as the locals in the 1930s called it during Joe's stay, the "Bruno Hotel." *Photograph taken by author.*

The rules of the Schuylkill County Prison in 1934 were simple and clear. First and foremost, of course, prisoners had to actually be confined in their cells. They had to wear prison uniforms. They had to rise at a certain time and turn lights out at a certain time. They could not meet visitors privately or in any place other than the area specifically designated for that purpose. They couldn't order food from the local grocer and prepare it in their own cells. And while all of these rules are reasonable means of controlling a prison population, neither Joe Bruno nor his co-conspirators were subject to any of them.

Before and during Joe's trials, he was a Schuylkill County Prison "trusty"—a prisoner to whom the warden and staff entrusted special privileges. Typically, trusties were nonviolent offenders whose sentences were winding down—men for whom disobeying prison rules would have been counterproductive to their goal of release. Trusties, for obvious reasons, were not suspected murderers with a presumed history of widespread criminal activity and the political leverage to have things done their way.

As was his skill, in prison, Joe found a fellow of like mind with whom he could forge an alliance. Sammy Stramara had been arrested three months earlier than Joe. The discovery of sixty-five stolen cars led police to conclude that Stramara, his brother and their accomplices were the ringleaders in an auto theft ring of surprisingly uncomplicated yet effective design. Stramara et al would purchase from their owners wrecked cars at unusually attractive prices. Once in possession of the cars—or, more importantly, their titles of ownership—the Stramaras substituted the junkers with stolen, more highly marketable models of the same make and color, according to investigators. The grand jury agreed with these allegations, and just six days prior to Bruno's incarceration, Stramara was charged with twenty-seven criminal counts, including receiving stolen goods, illegally altering motor vehicle identification and registration numbers and selling stolen vehicles. It was the largest number of counts returned by any Schuylkill County grand jury, and it wasn't finished yet. Come January 1935, forty-four more charges were expected.

Through an unspoken understanding, Joe Bruno and Sammy Stramara seemed to assume control of the jail. Both worked in the medical room, positions that offered great flexibility owing to the ostensible need to, at all hours of the day or night, attend to prisoners suffering from alcohol withdrawal. Neither Sammy nor Joe needed to abide by the standard rule that all prisoners had to be locked in their cells by 9:00 p.m. In fact, one prison employee recalled that the only time Joe's cell was ever locked was when he, himself, left it and wanted to protect its contents. This was the case, for instance, when Joe used the prison kitchen to make his own sauce and meals from ingredients ordered from and delivered by nearby Long's grocery market. And when they weren't cooking in the prison kitchen, Joe, Sammy and their associates were cooking in their own cells using electric stoves—twenty-six of which were subsequently removed from the cellblock where Stramara and the Bruno clan were incarcerated. There were even rumors that Joe had a mistress who came and went as she pleased.

Prison life was good for Joe's family, too. Brother Phil almost immediately assumed control of the prison barbershop and later the "candy store," proceeds from which he paid the warden a concession. Arthur Bruno delivered coal to the warden. Joe's son James worked as a clerk in the prison office—a position that offered him unfettered access to cell keys and the prison arsenal. Relative by marriage Tony Orlando worked in the kitchen.

None of them played by prison rules, even those regarding visitation. Regular visiting hours were clear: Monday, Tuesday, Wednesday, Friday and Saturday from 1:00 p.m. to 2:00 p.m.; Thursdays from either 9:00 a.m. to 11:00 a.m. or 1:00 p.m. to 3:00 p.m.; and Sundays were reserved for out-of-town visitors only. All visits were to take place under guard in what was called the consulting room. A screen served to separate prisoner from visitor. Joe's family, however (particularly daughter Antoinette Billig), seemed to come and go as freely as the warden. It was not unusual for Antoinette to meet privately with her father, telling guards they had "business" to transact. Bank books, legal documents and other financial papers were carried between daughter and father, with Antoinette taking the position that the documents she brought were no one's business but Joe's. She was not contradicted.

For a while, the gothic county jail did indeed seem to be Joe's castle on the hill, laughingly referred to by many townspeople as the Bruno Hotel. But Joe's fairy tale, whether or not he realized it, was coming to an abrupt, strange and unhappy ending.

Chapter 10

THE TRIALS

The year 1934 is a memorable one in the annals of American crime. In May, outlaws Bonnie and Clyde were killed in a hail of bullets while driving along a country road in Bienville Parish, Louisiana. In September, German immigrant Bruno Hauptmann was arrested and charged with kidnapping Charles Lindbergh's infant son. Though it may not have merited quite as much ink as either of these stories, the Kelayres Massacre shared front pages with the most notorious events of its era. And while the stories about the Brunos' trials also garnered national headlines the following year, locally, it was the *only* news anyone cared to read about.

Pennsylvania and New York were the first states in the nation to see commercially operated television networks, but this didn't happen until 1941—well after the Bruno trials had concluded. To follow reporting on the 1935 prosecution of Joe Bruno, Schuylkill County residents had two options: newspapers or radio. It was in Pennsylvania that the country's first daily newspaper, the *Pennsylvania Daily Packet and Advertiser*, started publication in 1784. The press was a large and powerful industry in the state, and at the time of the massacre, nineteen papers were published in Schuylkill County alone. Pennsylvania was also an early leader in the broadcasting industry. KDKA in Pittsburgh is regarded as the nation's first commercially licensed radio station. It went live in 1920 and still broadcasts today. But if people wanted to follow the trial of Joe Bruno firsthand rather than hear about it from reporters who didn't know the local juice, they could go see it for themselves at the Schuylkill County

A street view of Pottsville, circa 1938, showing its steep hills and clapboard houses.
Image from WPA Federal Art Project Photographs of Pennsylvania Coal Miners and Coal Mining Communities.

The Schuylkill County Courthouse, where the trials of Joseph J. Bruno and his kin were held. *Photograph taken by author.*

Courthouse. This latter option was the one that most curious locals exercised.

On January 5, 1935, the commonwealth announced that it was completely prepared to prosecute the Bruno gang on five counts of murder. In what may have been a case of "be careful what you wish for," all defendants were granted separate trials. This served only to prolong the case and make it far more costly.

Outgoing Pennsylvania attorney general William A. Schnader named a special prosecutor for the trial: Albert L. Thomas, a 1901 graduate of Allegheny College in Meadville and veteran litigator who had formerly served as Crawford County district attorney. Keen professionally, in written communication he displayed a familiar, sometimes quirky approach that included calling colleagues and others by nicknames. Co-prosecutor James J. Gallagher was "Jimmie." Schuylkill County detective Lewis D. Buono was "Lewie." Newly elected Pennsylvania attorney general Charles J. Margiotti was "Charley." Thomas was equally informal when it came to the Brunos, to whom he referred in correspondence by first name or, in the case of the younger men, "the boys" rather than as "Mr." or "Defendant."

In a 1937 letter to Detective Buono—which Thomas begins by addressing his as-yet lack of payment for the Bruno trials—he wanders freely to other topics, revealing to Buono wonderfully uncensored details and thoughts. Having entered a judicial election, Thomas says of his opponent:

> [He] *is unscrupulous, unqualified, but very energetic as well as disrespectful. He has been successful in ingratiating himself into the confidence of the women voters. He attends the church functions, the pie socials, and poses as a goody-goody—arch hypocrite, in other words.*

But Thomas was also clearly a sentimental man who told Buono:

> *Permit me to express to you my deepest sympathy in the loss of your father. I know how hollow words really are in times like this, but nevertheless I have found it gratifying to know that the sympathies of your friends are really with you. It takes away some of the loneliness. It seems to fill up the void.*

Unfortunately for the Brunos, this sympathy did not extend to accused killers, for Thomas pursued the case with emotional detachment.

Joe's first trial was called to order on January 7, 1935. He was charged with the murder of Frank Fiorella. The halls of the Schuylkill County Courthouse were packed. Sitting immediately in front of the jail, the courthouse, too, casts a daunting shadow downward onto the town of Pottsville. Operational since 1891, it is made of the same sandstone from which the prison was constructed—sturdy, permanent stuff intended to stand for centuries.

With his round, horn-rimmed glasses and neat appearance, Joe could have been an accountant or office clerk. He appeared each day in court in natty attire—usually a gray three-piece suit across the vest of which was draped the gold chain of a pocket watch. An elk's tooth hung from the chain as a charm. A penknife was attached to the end of the chain, and when nervous, Joe would twirl it in the air, let it wrap around his finger, unwind the chain and twirl it again. It was a habit he repeated endlessly.

In a well-distributed photograph of Joe leaving the courthouse with two guards, he looks as tall as the men flanking him. Closer inspection of the dark shot shows that Joe is standing one step higher than they are. In truth, Joe was just over five feet, six inches tall. His suit size, thirty-nine short, gives a true picture of his stature. His $8.50-per-pair Bostonian shoes (eight times the cost most people of the day paid for footwear) were size 8D. What Joe

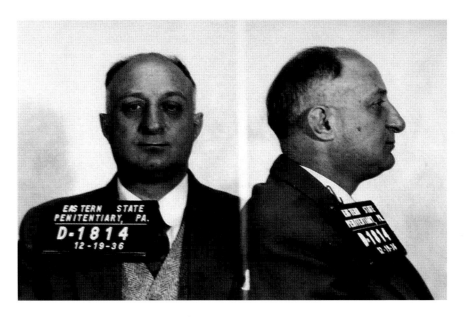

Joe Bruno's brother Phil poses for his mug shot. *Image from Schuylkill County Historical Society.*

lacked in stature, however, he made up for in demeanor, and throughout most of the trial, he remained stoic and seemingly unconcerned.

Joe's son James had his father's deceptively innocuous high hairline and long nose and face. In contrast, Joe's brother Phil's face was full and—especially owing to the permanent dark circle under his eyes—more intimidating.

Regardless of the heinousness of their alleged crimes, Joe and his clan were *causes célèbre*. Everyone had an opinion about the gang's guilt or innocence, and even imprisoned, the Bruno name still carried weight in the region. It was therefore not surprising that finding a jury for the trial of Joseph James Bruno was a laborious task—particularly since the prosecution sought the death penalty.

Approximately 150 prospective jurors were summoned to court on the first day of trial. One after another, they were dismissed by the attorneys. Judge Cyrus M. Palmer threatened to drag men and women in off the streets if the original panel was exhausted. Palmer, like the two other Schuylkill County Court of Common Pleas judges, was a Republican. Born in Pottsville and a lifelong resident, it would have been impossible for him not to know of the Brunos' reputation in the area. Two days after making it, his threat to find random replacements became a reality. Attorneys depleted the entirety of the pool before seating a jury, and Palmer sent sheriffs into the

Bullets found in the Bruno garage during the investigation of the massacre. It was just one of the many hiding places in which ammunition was scattered throughout the home. *Photograph taken by author at Schuylkill County Historical Society.*

court hallways and city streets to find new prospects. Finally, after a week of building frustration and anticipation, the jury was empanelled and the trial began in earnest.

An early volley fired by chief defense counsel John B. Stevens concerned the weapons recovered in the investigation. The prosecution wanted to enter them into evidence en masse. Stevens objected. Some of the guns, he argued, were found days after the initial search. Thomas countered that the cache of weapons proved premeditation on the Brunos' part and should be entered as one exhibit. Palmer ruled that the guns could all be entered into evidence but that this had to be done one at a time. Looking back, introducing these exhibits one at a time likely served to even more effectively illustrate to the jury the firepower stockpiled in Joe's home.

Sam Mascarelli took the stand on January 14. He was the first witness to testify to Joe Bruno's participation in the ambush. He spoke before an overflowing courtroom, and try as it might, the defense could not shake

Mascarelli from his story. "Bruno was leaning at the window with a gun in his hand," he said. After witnessing two flashes of gunfire, Mascarelli said he saw two men fall: Frank Fiorella and Dominic Perna.

A later witness, Jenni Tortanessi, whose broken English served as comic relief, nonetheless supported Mascarelli's story. Her testimony—like the letters written by Albert L. Thomas—bore the hallmarks of familiarity with the defendants. Phil Bruno's son was "Philly's boy." She knew the Bruno women and corrected the attorneys on their relationships to Joe or his family. While her command of the English language may have been lacking, her certainty about what she saw was unflappable. When asked if she was sure she had witnessed Joe and Phil shooting out of the window of Joe's home, Jenni adamantly answered, "Yes, sir."

Beatrice Fudge was one of the rare souls who spoke to the shooters during the massacre. As she and her three children reached the intersection of Centre and Fourth Streets, she heard shots coming from the lawn between the homes

The tattered American flag carried in the parade by twenty-one-year-old Carl Vacante. Close inspection reveals numerous holes made by shotgun pellets. Circles drawn in blue ink made the pellet holes easier for the jury to spot. *Photograph taken by author at Pennsylvania State Police Historical, Educational and Memorial Center.*

of Joe and James Bruno. Drawing nearer, she saw James firing a pistol. "Ain't you ashamed of yourself to shoot in between children like that?" she asked. As she tried to backtrack to Centre Street, Beatrice noticed a long gun sticking out of the window of Joe's home. There was a sound of breaking glass, and then shots could be heard coming from Joe's Fourth Street bedroom windows. She described the bullets as flying like hailstones.

Three men testified to hearing Joe make threats against the parade marchers well before the parade began. This testimony was buttressed by an emotional Samuel Fiorella, who told jurors that he, too, heard Bruno—speaking in Italian—say of the marchers that he would "get them all, one by one." Thomas concluded his questioning by asking Samuel Fiorella to describe his relationship to Frank Fiorella. In a breaking voice, the thirty-one-year-old witness replied, "He was my daddy."

Emil Cesario, an employee of the Haddock Mining Company, came forward to discredit the testimony of these four men, but especially considering Phil's connection to the colliery, prosecutors were suspicious. "A check on this fellow is needed," wrote one of the prosecutors on a small slip of paper. "I will tell today Gowan or Christ, state police, about him."

In addition to eyewitnesses, prosecutors benefited greatly from the records of the police who investigated the murders. One surviving note, assumed to be handwritten by Detective Buono, succinctly identifies the law enforcement officers involved in the case:

> *To Lt. Edwin Griffiths, State Police Barracks, West Reading, Pa., and along with you all of the written reports or investigations made on the evening of November 5—34 and subsequent thereto relative to the investigations into the riot, affray or killings which occurred...at Kelayres, Sch. Co.—Penna., in your possession or located at the State Police Barracks, West Reading, Pa. or any other place made by Troopers Soule, Lenker, Lowary, Sgt. Francis, Corporal Carr, Troopers or Clerks Smith, Ely, Sauer and Harve and anyone else.*

This note matches portions of the personnel lists of men serving in Troop C in Reading, Berks County, and Troop D in Wyoming, Luzerne County. Sergeant William W. Francis and Privates First Class John F. Lenker and George M. Sauer worked out of Reading. Corporal John A. Carr worked out of Wyoming. The other men, perhaps because of errors in surname spelling or rank, can't be positively identified.

From its very first witness to its forty-second, the prosecution's strategy was clear: to show that Joe had played an integral role in the massacre—not just that that he had actually killed Frank Fiorella but also that he had planned and instigated the whole thing.

Contrarily, the defense presented Joe as a worried husband and father—a man who was not only innocent but also the intended victim. In Joe's version of events, the family were all sitting together when they heard the rowdy parade march down the street toward their house. As the mob approached, according to Joe's rebuttal, they began hurling stones at the walls of the Bruno home. Shortly thereafter, the Brunos heard shots. At this point, Joe said he phoned the police to report his fear that the political parade was escalating into a home invasion. When the family heard more stones crash through their front windows, Joe ushered his frightened flock upstairs but remained on the first floor. The damage to the windows was not documented in the police photos found at the Schuylkill County Historical Society. However, there is no way to know if the exhibits donated by the county courthouse represent the totality of those presented to the jury.

In some respects, the trial was like a courtroom version of the Civil War. A number of members from the same family would testify. While half might take Joe's side, the other half hoped to help send him away.

When the prosecution rested, the defense presented its side. It soon became apparent to courtroom observers, reporters and, undoubtedly, the jury that the only witnesses called to rebut the prosecution's charges were Joe's family and the men and women who somehow benefited from him. Joe's counsel attempted to impugn Jenni Tortanessi's testimony by planting a seed in the jury's mind that her appearance was payback for the foreclosure on her home by the bank with which both James and Joe Bruno were associated. That theory did not seem to stick, nor did the statements by the sister of fellow prisoner Tony Orlando, who said it was not the Brunos but rather Michael Bevanko—a vocal opponent of the family—who fired some of the fatal shots. When asked by Prosecutor Gallagher how she could so positively identify one man out of the hundreds crowding the intersection, Mildred Cara explained that Bevanko, the supposed gunman, was standing directly under a streetlight, making him easy to spot. Another witness, Michael Kulish, also swore that Bevanko was the first to shoot. "I Michael Kulish," he wrote six days after the murders, "saw Michael Bevanko fire three shots to the home of J.J. Bruno before anybody else shot from the Bruno home." Contradicting Cara, however, Kulish said Bevanko was standing along a fence.

Joe's wife, Cecelia, was called on his behalf, a decision both Joe and his lawyers would come to regret. Under direct questioning by Joe's counsel, she told the jury that while everyone else in the house moved to the second floor during the shooting, Joe remained downstairs in his office, presumably calling the police. The implication of this testimony was clear: if Joe remained on the first floor, he could not possibly have fired at anyone from the second-story bedroom window. But under Gallagher's cross-examination, Cecelia contradicted this statement by saying that she herself was the only member of the family who stayed downstairs. By her third day on the stand, Cecelia's strain was evident. She seemed even smaller and paler than when she'd first taken the oath. Her hands fidgeted constantly throughout her questioning.

Another defense witness inflicting more harm than help was longtime housekeeper Annie Wishnefski. On the Saturday before the shooting, Wishnefski was upstairs in the "room that Joe slept [in]" and saw five guns propped against the radiator near the window. She described the guns as double-barreled. Wishnefski also saw a lard can under the dresser filled with shotgun shells and said there were other cartridges in the dresser drawers as well. Mrs. Bruno, sick and confined to bed, warned Wishnefski to be careful around the guns. When Wishnefski asked her why there were so many in the

The Salidago home sits diagonally across the intersection of Centre and Fourth Streets from the former Bruno home. The brick exterior still bears more than a dozen (now patched) bullet holes from the night of the Kelayres Massacre. *Photograph taken by author.*

home, Cecelia Bruno replied, "You know yourself that they are coming and bothering me. We have to protect ourselves."

Joe Bruno took the stand in his own defense. As he, in a sincere and quiet voice, pleaded his innocence, a familiar voice rang out. "Liar!" cried Jenni Tortanessi. After a swift and severe warning from the judge, she quieted herself for the remainder of the day's proceedings.

The former home of Frank Fiorella sits beside the Salidago property. *Photograph taken by author.*

On February 4, 1935, Judge Cyrus Palmer delivered a six-hour charge to the jury. He instructed jurors on the difference between murder and manslaughter and the varying degrees of both. By eleven o'clock that evening, there was still no verdict, so the jury was sequestered in the courthouse. Breakfast and lunch came and passed but still no decision.

Two days later, the prospect of a mistrial became tantalizingly real for Joe's team. One of the jurors, Mrs. John Connors, displayed symptoms of appendicitis. A doctor was called and announced to the judge that, in his professional opinion, she could continue deliberating without risk. The jury went back to work. The next day, sixty-five hours after they'd received the case, the jury had its decision.

Joe Bruno was found guilty of voluntary manslaughter in the death of Frank Fiorella.

Attorney General Charles J. Margiotti ran for governor in 1938 but dropped out of the race. His relationship with George H. Earle soured after Margiotti accused Earle's administration of mismanaging New Deal funds. *Image from* Smull's Legislative Hand Book and Manual of the State of Pennsylvania.

The penalty for this conviction was six to twelve years in prison; however, the sentence was immediately deferred pending Bruno's motion for a new trial.

Bruno told reporters that he should have been acquitted and that the only reason for the guilty verdict was the jurors' sympathy for Mrs. Connors. They reached an agreement only because she needed medical attention, he said. But Joe had little time to lament his first verdict, for his second trial would soon begin.

State attorney general Charles J. Margiotti wanted prosecutors to seek a venue change for the second trial. It was his belief that feeling ran so high in the Bruno case that finding an impartial jury was next to impossible. Unlike the first trial, in which he was defending a single charge, Joe Bruno was this time charged with three counts of murder. The families of Andrew Kostishion, Dominic Perna and John Galosky were all eager for their day in court.

Reluctantly, Albert L. Thomas complied with Margiotti's request and filed for a change of venue. When the Pennsylvania Supreme Court denied this request, Thomas was hardly distressed. Of the decision, he wrote:

> *The Supreme Court handed down an order in our application for change of venue denying our petition. They failed to consider any of the legal matters which might have some bearing upon our position. However, I am not disappointed as I never had any faith in the right of the Supreme Court to grant a change of venue on the application of the Commonwealth.*
>
> *The order…appoints Honorable Benjamin R. Jones, of the Eleventh Judicial District, to sit in Schuylkill County and try these cases on the first Monday of May, 1935. They further ordered that in the event the regular panel of jurors is exhausted…the court will designate [officials] to select additional jurors.*

While bringing an out-of-county arbiter to Schuylkill to try the case reduced worries of judicial partiality, the jurors would still be locals. Of this possible prejudice, Thomas was far more wary. In a letter to co-counsel, he advised:

> *We should have a thorough check made of the jury now summoned and we should take every precaution to guard this panel. The slightest evidence of an attempt to tamper with this jury should be carefully run down and arrests made where there is any evidence to sustain the action.*

Thomas's concerns about jury tampering were not without foundation. Two weeks after the first trial ended, a man named Ervin Daubert was arrested and held on $2,000 bail. He was accused of attempting to persuade two jurors to hold out for acquittal if they made it past voir dire and were chosen to serve. Neither juror was selected, but that did not negate the tampering threat.

In March 1935, Joe Bruno and his other jailed family members and associates petitioned to be released on bail. They argued that, in keeping with Pennsylvania law, they could not be incarcerated for more than two court terms without being tried. Their petition failed since the delay was a direct result of the change of venue petition.

In the second trial, the prosecution once again sought the death penalty. More than eighty witnesses were called by the state, just slightly more than were called by the defense. The prosecution took only four days to present its case. Judge Benjamin R. Jones, the Luzerne County judge brought in to preside over the trial, left no doubt that this was exactly the kind of expeditious approach he expected. Jones even volunteered to hold late afternoon sessions if it meant the case could keep moving.

Many of the same cast of characters from the first trial appeared before the jury. Some, though, were barred from repeat performances. These devalued witnesses included, in the words of prosecutor Thomas, "the dapper little McAloose who boasted about his picture being in the paper and some of the others who added nothing to our case."

On May 15, 1935, a jury of eleven men and one woman found Joe Bruno guilty of three counts of second-degree murder in the deaths of Kostishion, Perna and Galosky. Each count drew a penalty of ten to twenty years in prison. Again, the sentencing was deferred pending appeal.

Joe Bruno took the verdicts in stride. His daughter, Antoinette Billig, descended into hysteria and was helped from the courtroom.

Less than two months later, Joe's brother Phil was convicted of manslaughter in the deaths of Fiorella, Kostishion, Perna and Galosky. The other defendants were acquitted on these charges.

By the commencement of the third and final trial—this one for the murder of William Forke—there was much gamesmanship afoot between the lawyers themselves and between the prosecutors and county officials. In early July 1935, Schuylkill County commissioners made public the cost of the Bruno prosecution: an estimated $75,000 (more than $1 million by today's valuation). And this figure would only grow with the announcement of perjury charges against three witnesses in Joe's second trial. (Mildred Cara, William Chevinsky and Ben Festa were all charged with giving testimony in direct contradiction to that given during Joe's first trial.) The clear reason for the revelation of the bill of fees was to dampen the public's enthusiasm for continued prosecution, but wily attorney Albert L. Thomas recognized the ploy for what it was. In a letter to co-counsel James J. Gallagher, Thomas wrote:

> [Pennsylvania Attorney General Charles J. Margiotti] *stated that* [Bruno defense attorney] *Bechtel was in his office for the purpose of talking to him about a discharge of all defendants on the remaining charge.* [Margiotti] *called me up and asked my opinion. Bechtel reported to him that there was a very marked change in the sentiment toward us since our bill for fees had been presented thereby leading* [Margiotti] *to believe that our chances on another trial would not be as favorable as in the past...I*

was really surprised to see that Charley [Margiotti] *would entertain such reasons...I told him I had learned from Lewie* [Buono] *that the public sentiment was very strong in the condemnation of the jury's* [acquittal of all defendants except Joe and Phil Bruno] *in the last case, and that in my opinion our chances against Joe and Philip, and possibly three of the boys, would be much better than in the last trial.*

If prosecutors harbored any uncertainties at all, they concerned the cases against Paul and Arthur Bruno. Wrote Thomas:

I mentioned trying Joe [for a third time] *thinking they would possibly make some offer on the boys rather than to have them wait any longer for trial. I believed we all agreed that we should nol pros the case at least as to Paul and possibly Arthur. The* [defense attorneys] *have not made an application for discharge contrary to my expectations...I cannot see any disadvantage on their part in making such an application, and I am inclined to think Judge Jones would grant it.*

When questioned by defense counsel on his intentions for the third trial, Thomas was equally matter-of-fact:

As you know there is but one case remaining and that is the case against all seven defendants for the killing of William Forke. The Court has granted a severance for each defendant. Therefore, the Commonwealth, as the record now stands, is bound to call for trial a case against one defendant at a time, unless you withdraw your application for severance and consent to try them together. This is a matter entirely within your control.

This time, the defense agreed to do just that.

On September 13, 1935, a jury was empanelled one final time to hear the case against Joe Bruno and his six co-defendants on the charge of the murder.

Although transcriptions of the trial proceedings have gone missing over the years, notes from the investigation and depositions indicate that James was the shooter positively identified by the largest number of witnesses to the event. Unlike Joe and Phil, who shot unarmed victims from the relative anonymity of a second-floor bedroom window, an enraged James stood out in the open. Again and again, victims and bystanders described his flagrant actions. Surely, defense counsel was hard-pressed to combat the emphatic testimony of witnesses who swore they'd seen James, manic and infuriated, running back and forth in his own front yard while randomly firing his pistol.

In his own defense, James said it was just a coincidence that he was in possession of a gun the night of the shooting. It had been payday at the bank several days previously, he explained. He carried the gun to protect himself after picking up the money from the post office. After that, he had placed it in the side pocket of his car and forgotten about it. As he walked toward his father's house on the night of the parade, James stated that he heard shouts of: "There goes a Bruno!" and "Let him have it!" When marchers began throwing stones at his father's home, he retrieved the gun and yelled back, "What the hell do you people mean by this?" According to James, he only fired into the air in an attempt to frighten the hooligans away.

Under cross-examination, James Bruno was asked about a statement he made to the police the night of the massacre. "I never carried a gun in my pocket," he originally said. "I handled my father's gun and never took a chance in carrying it." When prosecutors in the third trial asked about these original statements, James replied, "I don't remember saying that."

In Paul Bruno's case, by contrast, there was far less firsthand, reliable evidence to prove he participated in the shooting. One witness, Mario Perna—brother of murdered Dominic Perna—testified that he saw gunfire coming from Paul's apartment window; however, he could not clearly identify the figure holding the weapon. Like Alfred Bruno, Paul was seen handling a revolver and ammunition in the bedroom of Joe Bruno's home, but there are no clear indications of the use of that weapon.

Although the family of William Forke was the last to find justice, this would be the only first-degree murder conviction Joe would receive for his participation in the Kelayres Massacre. The jury also found Joe's brother Phil guilty of murder in the first degree. Joe's sons James and Alfred were found guilty of murder in the second degree, as were Phil's son Arthur, Paul Bruno and Tony Orlando. Again, sentencing was suspended on appeal. In fact, it would take nearly two years for these men to learn their fates.

In the end, it was left to the judge to determine how each man would be punished, and on July 13, 1936, it seemed that the final chapter was written for the Bruno clan. Joe and Phil received life sentences. Alfred, James and Tony each received ten to twenty years. Arthur received five to ten years. Paul was the only defendant to be granted a new trial.

The town of Kelayres breathed a collective sigh of relief. The horrific events of election eve 1935 were finally behind them. At least, that's what they thought.

Chapter 11

THE LEGEND OF LEWIS BUONO BEGINS

Lewis D. Buono was born in Philadelphia in 1893 to parents Felice and Evangelista. At age two, he and his family moved to Chester, a town in Delaware County. From an early age, Buono was a high achiever, especially when it came to anything involving competition. In high school, Buono played (and excelled at) both football and baseball, even playing on several semiprofessional baseball teams.

At age seventeen, Buono enlisted in the army. He served in the cavalry, which, in turn, made him eligible for gubernatorial appointment to the mounted Pennsylvania constabulary. After that, he worked as an investigator for Pennsylvania's Office of the State Fire Marshal.

Buono's self-confidence was evident in the way he carried himself. Even under the most tense of situations, he seemed completely at ease with the ankle of one leg resting on the knee of the other, his large hands lying motionless in his lap. Buono's face was full and healthy, and the strong "V" of his hairline stood out above his broad forehead.

From his first days in law enforcement onward, Buono's reputation was that of a man who latched on to the trail of a criminal like a dog to a bone. The first well-known example of this was Buono's work on a horse-theft ring headed by a devious con named Schmoyer, who worked throughout eastern Pennsylvania. In 1910, the case was assigned to Sergeant Harvey J. Smith of C Troop. Smith tracked Schmoyer mercilessly until December 1912, when he finally found the thief—incarcerated in New York for the very same crime. Although three witnesses from Pennsylvania identified Schmoyer as having stolen their horses, requests for detainer were ignored by the State of New York, and Schmoyer was paroled. He immediately violated the conditions of his parole by leaving the state and going back to Pennsylvania—and to his thieving ways.

In September 1915, a Schuylkill County farmer called the state police at C Troop to report that he had spotted a man bearing a striking resemblance to Schmoyer. This time, Trooper Buono was assigned the case. Along with another trooper by the name of Stillwell, Buono picked up Schmoyer's trail and followed it on horseback for more than thirty miles before traveling the final few miles by motorcar. Just before midnight, Buono did what his predecessor had not: he captured and arrested Schmoyer in the act of accepting payment for a horse and buggy he'd stolen in Lancaster County.

Buono's legend grew when, four years later, he single-handedly tracked and captured an arsonist named Leonard Rundell. Rundell had conspired with the owner of a five-and-dime in Bradford County to burn the failing business and collect insurance proceeds. Not the sharpest of criminal minds, Rundell told a widow living on the second floor of the building the owner's plans. The mother of three young children, the widow kept vigil out of fear that she and her family might be burned alive. On the night of May 16, 1918, the widow detected the overpowering smell of kerosene and called the police, who broke into the first-floor storeroom in time to prevent the blaze. Rundell was arrested but released on bail and, in keeping with his pattern, shortly thereafter fled the state. In November of that year, the case was assigned to investigator Lewis D. Buono, who, after persistent detective work, concluded that Rundell was in Los Angeles working in a department store.

Buono's first course of action was to ask local California police to arrest his fugitive. Unfortunately, they reported back to Buono that they failed to locate Rundell. Convinced that his theory was right, Buono traveled to California himself. Bradford County, believing Buono to be chasing the proverbial wild goose, announced it would not pay the expenses for his trip.

Almost immediately upon his arrival in Los Angeles, Buono found and arrested Rundell at the very department store he'd told local police to visit. When he returned to Pennsylvania by train, escapee in hand, Bradford County's sheriff paid Buono's full tab.

Several years later, Buono left the fire marshal's office to take the job as Schuylkill County's chief detective. Ironically, he became a colleague to Joseph J. Bruno, who held the title of deputy detective, although no records have been found of Joe's actual service in this capacity. When the Kelayres

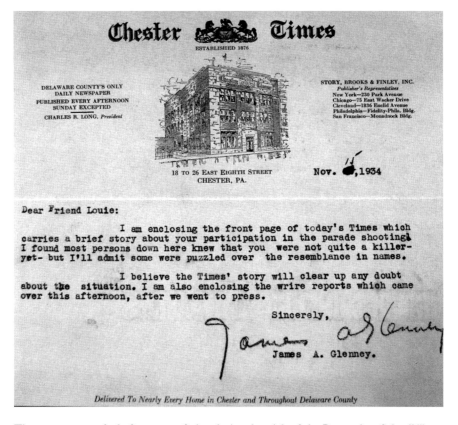

There was a great deal of name confusion during the trials of the Bruno clan. Schuylkill County detective Louis Buono's name was often confused with the man he investigated. And both Lewis Buono and Joe Bruno's names appeared on the same newspaper pages as Bruno Hauptmann—on trial at the same time for the Lindbergh baby kidnapping. *From Schuylkill County Historical Society.*

Massacre occurred, Buono must have—if only for a short and private time—worried about investigating his fellow law enforcement officer. If he went at it too hard, it would appear as if Buono bore a grudge. If he went too soft, the community would believe Buono was just another of Bruno's patronizing cronies. In the end, he investigated the case as he would any other: with determination, professionalism and integrity.

When the story first hit the newspapers, the similarity of the surnames "Bruno" and "Buono" created some concern among the residents of Lewis Buono's hometown. Several careless reporters and editors had inadvertently interchanged the killer's name with the detective's. In a personal note to Buono on newspaper letterhead, *Chester Times* editor James A. Glenney wrote:

I am enclosing the front page of today's Times *which carries a brief story about your participation in the parade shooting. I found most persons down here knew that you were not quite a killer—yet—but I'll admit some were puzzled over the semblance in names. I believe the* Times *story will clear up any doubt about the situation.*

If Schuylkill County officials hired Buono based on what he'd accomplished *prior* to his arrival, they had much more to learn. Buono would prove capable of even greater feats of investigation and detection. And unfortunately for the Brunos, these would come at the expense of Big Joe's freedom.

Chapter 12

JOE CHECKS OUT OF THE BRUNO HOTEL

In December 1936, Joe Bruno got the worst possible news: the Pennsylvania Supreme Court had denied his petition for retrial. This meant that he would be transferred from the familiar and comfortable Schuylkill County Prison to the austere and unyielding Eastern State Penitentiary in Philadelphia. Joe would be just another murderer at Eastern State. There would be no food deliveries from the local grocer, nor would he have the keys to his own cell. Big Joe found this prospect completely unacceptable.

At the jail in Pottsville, Bruno visitors were always less scrutinized than those of other prisoners. But just after the Supreme Court decision was handed down, a new and even more sweeping edict was issued by county commissioner Phil Ehrig. According to the sworn statement of Warden Herbert F. Gosselin, Ehrig made it quite clear that Joe's family—any or all of them—should be allowed to visit with Joe privately in the consulting room. In fact, all of the Brunos enjoyed increased visitation during the first half of that December. The wives of both Phil Bruno and Tony Orlando came almost daily, their visits held behind closed doors and out of earshot of the guards.

Without question, Joe's most frequent visitor was his daughter Antoinette. On December 17, 1936, however, she went to the jail an unprecedented four times. With each visit, she brought paperwork of a financial nature—items she told the guards were for her father's eyes only. They complied. The paperwork in question came mostly from an overflowing safety deposit box Joe rented at the Schuylkill Trust Company not far from the jail. The box was in three names: Joe's, Antoinette's and

Antoinette's sister Elveda's. Among the myriad documents it protected were life insurance policies, executed judgments against and between family members for thousands of dollars, stock certificates for companies including U.S. Rubber and Philadelphia Electric, notes for debts due, an employment agreement between Joe and a private investigator by the name of Harvey J. Smith (likely Lewis D. Buono's old police colleague), negotiable bonds and cash.

That same evening, Joe Bruno complained to Warden Gosselin of a toothache and asked to be taken to a dentist in Pottsville—the same dentist Phil Bruno, Arthur Bruno and Tony Orlando had also previously visited on several occasions. "That bridge is dropping on my jaw," Bruno said. "I'd like to have it fixed." It was not Joe's first complaint, and he had in fact seen the dentist several times previously. Gosselin replied that Bruno should speak to the deputy the next morning to make arrangements for the visit.

On December 18, 1936, Second Deputy Wilbur Hale witnessed the following:

> *I came to work about 9 o'clock and was there about fifteen minutes when Joe Bruno and "Speck" Irving went down to the dentist...Joe Bruno came out of his cell, which was No. 12. He had an overcoat over his arm... George Wallyung came in about two o'clock and asked if Joe Bruno was in. I told him he had gone to the dentist and not yet returned. The next thing, Bob Walker came in and said, "I believe Joe Bruno is gone." We talked a while and I said, "They were looking for trouble a long time, I guess they've got it."*

Hale's sworn statement seemed to support Gosselin's comments about the county commissioners. "When the Brunos' privileges were revoked by Warden Gosselin," he said, "they were restored by Commissioners Ehrig and Maurer."

First Deputy Robert Walker, to whom Hale refers, was not regarded kindly by the Brunos. Walker, a stickler for rules, would not allow Joe's family to get to the private area beyond the visitors' screen. An incensed Joe told Walker that he "wouldn't be there long." Like Hale and Gosselin, Walker felt Commissioner Ehrig took too active a role in intervening on the Brunos' behalf, going so far as to tell Walker directly, "I want the Brunos to have more privileges." Ehrig himself was one of Joe's most frequent visitors, according to Walker.

Joe's failure to return to jail after his dentist appointment was not reported to the warden or police for more than five hours. Guard Guy "Speck" Irving

This is the prison gate Joe should have exited when he left the Schuylkill County prison on his way to Eastern State Penitentiary. Instead, he took a quicker and far more interesting route. *Photograph taken by author.*

said he hadn't reported it sooner because he was conducting an exhaustive search of Pottsville in hopes of recapturing the convicted murderer. This peculiar decision is not the only unusual aspect of Irving's actions—or employment, for that matter.

At the time of Bruno's escape, there were only six guards working for the prison. Most of these men worked eight-hour daily shifts. The two deputies who served as part of the guard staff worked either 5:30 a.m. to 3:00 p.m. or, like Hale, 9:00 a.m. to 8:00 p.m. Speck Irving had only recently been added to the guard staff, but not by Warden Gosselin. Irving, whose mischievous smile and youthful good looks were enhanced by his narrow-brimmed, head-hugging cap, made the warden uneasy. "He is headstrong with a one-track mind," Gosselin said of Irving. "Not well educated but has done a little police work." Gosselin himself had a man in mind for the open position, one who had experience as a prison guard. He was overruled by the county commissioners, who hired Irving and told him to report to the prison on December 8, 1936—ten days prior to Bruno's escape. Irving himself admitted that he had "not asked for that particular job" but likely received it because several of the commissioners were his friends.

But while Gosselin may have found Irving's hire suspect, the warden had his own decisions to answer for, not the least of which was how the Brunos were able to wear and keep street clothes in their cells. When Joe left for the dentist, he, as Hale stated, had an overcoat over his arm, but that arm—like the rest of Joe—was attired in a gray wool suit, hardly standard prison uniform.

Had Joe left a few minutes later, he would have had yet another visit from daughter Antoinette. According to guard Handel Tonkin, she returned to the prison carrying a bankbook identifiable as one given by the Schuylkill County Trust. Antoinette told Tonkin she wanted to see her father. When Tonkin explained that he'd already left for the doctor, Antoinette asked what doctor. Tonkin told her he didn't know. For a moment, she considered leaving the bankbook with Tonkin with instructions to give it to Joe. She subsequently changed her mind, saying there was too much in the book for him to see. Instead, Antoinette asked Tonkin to tell Joe Bruno that his daughter had been there and that she was going to Harrisburg to pick up her "kid brother" and bring him back home to Kelayres.

Speck Irving's version of the events leading up to Joe's escape was entertaining at best and woefully negligent at worst. At about 9:30 a.m., he said, he made the short drive to the dentist's office. He carried no firearm or club, and Joe was not restrained. In fact, Joe traveled in the front seat. Irving drove down Second Street to Race Street and then to Centre Street, where the dentist's office was located, but once there, he found no open parking spaces. While double-parked on the street, Irving told Joe to exit the vehicle and head into the dentist's office. He said he would join Joe there as soon as he found a spot for the car. Irving swore that he later peered through the dentist's window and saw Joe in the chair undergoing treatment. But about 1:00 p.m., seeing no further sign of his charge, he became concerned.

For nearly two hours, said Irving, he drove around Pottsville searching for the missing prisoner. Just after 2:30 p.m., Irving gave up on the prospect of finding Joe and thought it best to share the bad news with his boss. Rather than place the call himself, however, he asked Bill Golden, owner of a local garage, to make the call for him. The call was answered by prison clerk Jack Holton, whose curious response was: "I better talk to Jimmy." "Jimmy" was Joe's son James, whose prison job was working in Holton's office. Shortly thereafter, James, who was freely roaming the corridor, remarked to First Deputy Walker: "Looks as if Joe Bruno is gone."

At about this same time, guard George Wallyung heard similar news through the prison grapevine. As Wallyung entered the prison office, Clerk Holton remarked that the newspapers had already gotten wind of the story. When Wallyung asked what story, the prison clerk replied, "Joe is gone."

By 3:00 p.m., Warden Gosselin had finally been apprised of the situation. He left the jail and, on the way to the police station, ran into District Attorney L.E. Enterline and Detective Buono. It was only then that the search for Joseph J. Bruno—and the investigation into how he was able to so easily escape—officially began.

Meanwhile, Speck Irving, squarely responsible for losing a convicted murderer, was telling everyone who might listen that he was as surprised as anyone to find Joe missing when he returned from parking the car.

Chapter 13

ANATOMY OF AN ESCAPE

Antoinette Billig was Joe and Cecelia Bruno's second child. Born between sons James and Alfred, she was a fierce defender of her father and, according to rumors, took a more than casual interest in her father's business dealings. With both the family patriarch and eldest son behind bars, it was Antoinette who served as go-between and emissary for her jailed kin.

It took several days for investigators to piece together what exactly Antoinette had given Joe during their pre-escape visits. After thoroughly studying what was left of the contents of Joe's safety deposit box, they believed she gave her father roughly $1,000 in cash, plus a fistful of negotiable bonds. All totaled, Joe Bruno left jail with about $35,000. Apparently, Antoinette had hoped to give him other resources and information on the morning of the escape, but Joe left for the dentist before she could make good on those plans.

Within hours of the escape, Lewis D. Buono began questioning employees of the jail, including the warden and guards. At the same time, police were following up on a variety of tips, including the reported sighting of a plane landing at an airport twenty miles north of Pottsville at about the same time Joe disappeared. Once again, Governor Earle would be drawn into the Kelayres Massacre, and he, in turn, would assign Pennsylvania attorney general Charles J. Margiotti to aid in Buono's investigation. The day after the escape, the two men continued their interviews, also taking statements from the county commissioners. Buono and Margiotti would soon learn that the soap opera–like machinations of these supposed civil servants nearly eclipsed their lapses in judgment. Warden Herbert F. Gosselin's statement

WANTED FOR ESCAPE FROM PRISON
WAS UNDER SENTENCE OF THREE LIFE
TERMS ON CHARGES OF MURDER

$1000 REWARD!

JOSEPH J. BRUNO, Italian-American; 52 yrs., 5 ft. 6½ in., 150 lbs., medium build, med. dark complex., thin black hair graying at temples, smooth face and dark beard.

Long prominent nose. Round shouldered and walks with head slightly inclined downward. In upper jaw on left side has a double tooth bridge with gold crown on first molar with dummy tooth attached posteriorly to the first molar. In lower jaw on left side has a large two-surfaced silver filling in the lower first molar.

When last seen was wearing medium dark grey suit, salt and pepper topcoat, gray felt hat and black shoes. Had gold watch with Elk Tooth charm, usually worn

JOE BRUNO

JOE BRUNO

across vest. Will wear or have on person dark tortoise-shell glasses as shown in photo on right. Has relatives and friends in New York, Phila., Detroit, Port Huron, Denver, Wheeling, Toledo, Pottstown and Reading. Escaped from jail at Pottsville, Penna., December 18, 1936, while awaiting transfer to Eastern Penitentiary.

If located hold and notify LEWIS D. BUONO, Chief of County Detectives,
Pottsville, Pennsylvania,
or Pennsylvania State Police, Harrisburg, Pa.

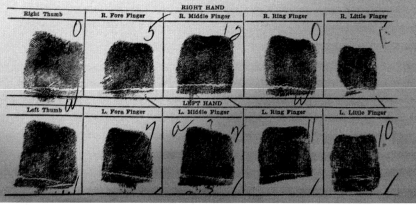

A wanted poster created for Joseph J. Bruno after his escape from the Schuylkill County prison. *Image from Schuylkill County Historical Society.*

well illustrates the backstabbing and attempts at self-preservation through which investigators were forced to wade:

> *Gosselin: After thinking this whole situation over, I believe there has been a conspiracy* [at the prison] *to overthrow me…I had nothing to do with the guards whatsoever. That power was taken away from me. Commissioner Ehrig was antagonistic to every move I made. There are letters…in the Commissioners' file requesting improvements to the prison that were tabled.*
>
> *Margiotti: Requesting what?*
>
> *Gosselin: Improvements in the prison that were tabled…There were three guards, Irving, Kats and Sweeney, who for the past five months—no, the past three months, I will say, have been carrying on a whispering campaign. They neglected their work. They should be over here at the court house…All of these things lead me to believe, General Margiotti, that I have been the victim of something I didn't realize.*
>
> *Margiotti: Well, now, what?*
>
> *Gosselin: I think I was the victim of a nice little frame-up.*
>
> *Margiotti: How?*
>
> *(Mr. Gosselin shakes his head.) Gosselin: I don't believe they wanted me there.*
>
> *Margiotti: Well, then, they could have fired you?*
>
> *Gosselin: They were afraid of the fire from the minority commissioner, I guess, and the general public.*
>
> *Margiotti: Well, would they go to the extent of instigating any conspiracy to permit Bruno to escape?*
>
> *Gosselin: I won't go that far…*

It appears that Gosselin's strategy for evading responsibility was twofold: to blame the commissioners for the poor security arrangements for Joe Bruno's dentist appointment and to rely on the fact that his knowledge of the escape came, for all practical purposes, too late to really do anything about it. In his sworn statement, Gosselin said that, upon hearing from Speck Irving that Joe Bruno had taken off, his directive to Irving was "go and get him," not the most specific of commands.

The commissioners were more forthcoming if hardly more helpful when interviewed by Margiotti and Buono. Commissioners Paul Ehrig and Alvin Maurer both admitted to telling Gosselin to let the Bruno women freely visit Joe, but Ehrig was emphatic that he never insisted they be left alone with Joe where guards could not see them.

*Ehrig: Who in the world would ever expect that a man of his experience…
would ever permit these women to go in there and closet themselves up with
Joe Bruno, without a guard over them, watching them? Who in the world
would ever expect that he was permitting the women and Bruno to be in
a consultation room all by themselves, with the door closed? I would never
expect that. I expected that when these women went back there, the guards
would look after the situation, and wouldn't permit anything to be done
that might bring about the escape of Bruno, or that they would hand him
anything he shouldn't have.*

Regardless of the he said/he said game played among the prison staff
and commissioners, on December 19, 1936, Judge Roy B. Hicks charged
Herbert Gosselin, Robert Walker, Guy Irving and Antoinette Billig with a
menu of charges, including willful aid to an escape, conspiracy to facilitate
an escape and providing money to a convicted murderer. Each of the four
was held on $15,000 bail. Gosselin was bailed out immediately.

The county commissioners posted a $1,000 reward to anyone who could
return Joe Bruno to their prison.

Meanwhile, it was Joe's family—left behind at the Schuylkill County
Prison—who received perhaps the harshest of consequences: they were all
immediately transferred to Philadelphia's Eastern State Penitentiary, the
place where Joe himself was set to transfer the day following his escape.

On December 21, Margiotti accused the county commissioners of
hampering efforts to investigate Joe Bruno's jailbreak. They were, he charged,
prohibiting investigators to interview prisoners unless the commissioners'
own attorneys were present. Two days later, warrants went out for the two
Republican commissioners, Ehrig and Maurer, for acting as accessories
after the fact of a murder. Ehrig left town, but Maurer turned himself
in to Alderman Robert Kalbach. Bail for both men was set at $15,000.
Democratic commissioner James Campion was believed to have played a
role in the escape.

Judge Hicks, for reasons lost to history, increased Antoinette Billig's bail
from $15,000 to $15,500—a sum subsequently raised by four Kelayres
residents. She was released from county prison on Christmas Eve. By
now, there were rumors of unrest among the formerly united Bruno front.
Surely, Joe's kin would have been equally keen on a Christmas outside of
prison walls.

The big question, of course, concerned Joe's whereabouts. Law
enforcement in states surrounding Pennsylvania was active in the search.

But Joe's connections were widespread. Had he gone west to California? Perhaps to Mexico, where American investigators could not easily search for him? Did he go to Italy? There were stories that he had consulted attorneys about that country's extradition laws.

Buono and Margiotti believed that Bruno had been planning his escape for months and that he had sufficient assets to remain on the run for an indefinite amount of time. The truth was, Joe Bruno could afford to go anywhere. Worse, he had a huge head start.

Chapter 14

FRANK MILLER COMES HOME

The New Year was rapidly approaching, and still Schuylkill County officials had no idea where Joe Bruno was hiding. Attorney General Charles J. Margiotti, openly unhappy about the seemingly endless shadow the Bruno case cast on his public persona, blamed the escape on a well-planned conspiracy. Antoinette Billig denied any involvement in planning her father's escape. She suggested to investigators that he probably just left on a whim while visiting the dentist. James J. Gallagher, one of the special prosecutors during the Bruno trials, asserted that Bruno was communicating with family member by means of specially coded telegraph messages, a charge the family also denied.

Detective Lewis D. Buono headed up the daily investigation, including sending out wanted notices and responding to numerous tipsters who—in exchange for the reward, of course—promised to tell him exactly where he could find Big Joe.

Joe Bruno's wanted posters were simple and to the point, usually showing him in two poses: one with glasses and one without. "Wanted for escape from prison," read the headline of one, "was under sentence of three life terms on charges of murder." Anyone reading the poster probably did a double take. The man in the photos looked more like a mortician than a murderer.

Buono included all of the pertinent details the poster size would allow:

JOSEPH J. BRUNO, Italian-American; 52 yrs., 5 ft. 6½ in., 150 lbs., medium build, med. dark complexion, thin black hair graying at temples, smooth face and dark beard. Long, prominent nose. Round shouldered and walks with head slightly inclined downward. In upper jaw on left side has a double tooth bridge with gold crown on first molar with dummy tooth attached posteriorly to the first molar. When last seen was wearing medium dark gray suit, salt and pepper topcoat, gray felt hat and black shoes. Had gold watch with elk tooth charm, usually worn across vest. Will wear or have on person dark tortoise-shell glasses as shown in the photo on right. Has relatives and friends in New York, Phila., Detroit, Port Huron, Denver, Wheeling, Toledo, Pottstown and Reading. Escaped from jail at Pottsville, Penna., December 18, 1936, while awaiting transfer to Eastern State Penitentiary. If located hold and notify Lewis D. Buono, Chief of County Detectives, Pottsville, Pennsylvania.

In communicating with fellow law enforcement officers, Buono created a document entitled "Additional Data Relative to Description of J.J. Bruno." It offered even more personal details, including hat size (65/8), shirt size (fifteen-inch neck, thirty-three-inch sleeve), underwear size (forty short) and even the kind of ties he wore (moiré and paisley.) The description goes on to include:

Subject purchased clothing from Doutrich's at Pottsville.
Subject purchased Stetson and Lee hats at prices varying from $3.25 to $7.00.
Subject wears Manhattan Silk Shirts with Van Jack collars, pays $5.00 for shirts.
Subject has white gold watch (make unknown). Yellow gold chain with long links, and penknife on end of chain.
Subject uses glasses for reading only, seldom wears them on the street.

As of April 10, 1937, the reward for the return of Joe Bruno had reached $1,200. When responding to informants believing they had information on Joe's whereabouts, Buono both encouraged and promised confidentiality. In a letter of response to one possible lead from Ontario, Buono wrote:

I will see that you get the entire [$1,200 reward] if your information is correct. You will not have to divide it with anyone and no one will be able to take it from you if you will work with me confidentially and do as I say. First I will promise you that I will not pass this information along to any other police and it shall be a secret between you and me. You can also trust *me that I will never give you away or tell anyone living near you where I got my information. If after you have checked your information and you think it is Joseph Bruno, write to me and tell me all you have found out and I will come to see you any place that you want to see me. The reason I say the secret is to be between you and me is because if more people know about it you might have to divide the reward with them, but only if us two know about it then you will get the entire reward. I cannot claim any of the reward because I get my salary from the county.*

…If it appears the man is Joseph Bruno I will come to see you. Don't forget to send me all the information you have as this is very important. Do this as quickly as possible so that if the man is Joseph Bruno, we can get up there before he moves to some other town.

While Buono was fielding tips, Schuylkill County Prison officials and employees were defending themselves in court. On May 15, 1937, Guy "Speck" Irving was convicted of negligence in permitting Joe Bruno to escape. As part of its verdict, the jury recommended to the judge extreme mercy when it came to sentencing. Either way, Irving was expected to file a motion for a new trial.

Robert Walker was also found negligent in the escape. Warden Herbert Gosselin was acquitted of the charge of willfully permitting Bruno to flee.

In addition to responding to correspondence, Buono also worked in the field. He spent endless hours tracking leads. Buono believed that Joe Bruno had been living in New York City since his escape. This was his geographic area of focus. In tales told since the escape, Buono is described as a man possessed—one who traveled to New York each evening by car, worked the streets in plain and tramp-like clothes and gathered information from anyone who might know Joe Bruno's whereabouts. To throw off suspicion of anyone who might notice his arrivals and departures, he replaced his Pennsylvania license plate with one from New York, reversing the process when he again crossed state lines on the way back to Pottsville.

While law enforcement from varying states and agencies searched for him, Joe Bruno was, if his correspondence is to be believed, traveling and trying to decide where he would ultimately settle down. In an undated letter to his wife, Cecelia, purportedly composed while he hid in Havana, Cuba, Joe wrote:

After plenty of worrying I decided to write to you and let you know I am well and have already made arrangements to leve [sic] for South America, you will hear from me later.

Very sorry all of this had to happen without aney folt [sic] of mine but I want you above all to take care of yourself and everything. I understand it is an awful strain on your mind but we will have to make the best of it. I will write to Antoinetta [sic] when I get there.

Yours,

J.J.

Clearly, mentions of Havana and South America could well have been red herrings he hoped investigators would follow. And one can't help but ponder whether Joe's comment about his lack of culpability is—at least in his own view—sincere or rather meant to taunt the police who might eventually read the letter. Either way, it seems callous to tell the wife whom he'd abandoned and shamed to "make the best of" life in harsh Kelayres while he speaks of traveling to the sunny locales of Florida, California and tropical Cuba. At the time, Cuba and the United States had a close political and economic relationship, and many wealthy Americans vacationed there. It is not infeasible for Joe to have visited—although the brevity of his time on the lam makes this claim suspect. It appears that Lewis Buono's instincts were correct and that Joe spent most of his days on the run in New York City.

The facts of Joe's escape and whereabouts are far less interesting than the wild theories. On the morning of December 18, 1936, when Joe was supposed to go to the dentist, he instead ducked into a waiting car driven by Joshua Nilo. Nilo, a longtime Bruno friend and likely business associate, worked as a barber. His associate, Rocco Garramone, had ties to a Hazleton nightclub called the Cotton Club and, in some news reports, is said to have had some connection to the 1938 "Flag Day" massacre in Hometown. Initially, Joe stayed in Garramone's Hazleton home. Four days later, the two men drove Bruno to New York City, where he established a new identity as Frank Miller.

It is quite possible that Joe Bruno's "disguise" was the least effective ruse in criminal history. Its full extent included dying his gray hair black, growing a mustache (which he also dyed black), gaining twenty pounds and exchanging tortoise-shell glasses for rimless lenses. Nonetheless, Bruno successfully hid for nearly eight months in an apartment in the Upper East Side before being rearrested.

Bruno's capture was remarkably unsensational. A tip led cops to Bruno's hideout. Detective Buono, state police superintendent Lynn G. Adams and a number of New York City patrolmen went to the apartment building where Joe was staying, but he was not home. They waited on the sidewalk for Joe to return. As Joe approached, he surely knew what was about to happen, yet he didn't attempt to flee or evade his fate. In fact, he appeared almost relieved. When asked to identify himself, Joe pointed to Detective Buono, whom he'd known for years, and said, "Ask that fellow there."

Joe appeared in a New York court wearing a suit whose description sounds very similar to that of the one he had worn when he escaped. He waived all extradition proceedings and willingly went with Buono, who placed himself between his old nemesis and the frantic press. "He is more content now than he was as a fugitive," Buono reportedly said, the only public statement he made regarding the arrest.

Although he was believed to have $35,000 in cash and other liquid assets, Joe's pockets contained just $9. A thorough search of his apartment revealed no additional funds.

Attorney General Charles J. Margiotti took credit for the rearrest of Joe Bruno, saying that the tip that led to the New York City hideout came directly to him. Those who know Lewis D. Buono had other thoughts on who the true detective was when it came to finding Big Joe.

On August 23, 1937, a crowd numbering in the several hundreds lined the streets to watch police escort Joe Bruno inside Eastern State Penitentiary, where he joined five other family members. Detective Buono and Corporal Jacob Hess of the state motor police had left New York just before lunchtime. By 3:30 p.m., Joe was back behind bars.

Though its façade is similar to that of the Schuylkill County prison, the Brunos found Eastern State Penitentiary to be far less accommodating to their lifestyle. *From the* Eighty-Fifth Annual Report of the Inspectors of the State Penitentiary for the Eastern District of Pennsylvania for the Year 1914, *Philadelphia, 1915.*

The following October, the Schuylkill County commissioners (who had been exonerated of any culpability in the Bruno escape) awarded three New York detectives a $1,000 award for their part in recapturing Joe.

In a letter of thanks to a New Jersey officer who also assisted in Joe's capture, Schuylkill County district attorney L.E. Enterline wrote, "The apprehension of Bruno meant a great deal to this county, as his escape was a terrible blot upon its record."

Once Joe Bruno was back behind bars, with the exception of occasional short newspaper items about Bruno family pleas for pardons, it was as if history had swallowed the clan whole, leaving behind no trace of their once notorious actions.

Chapter 15

THE AFTERMATH

In total, nine men died during the November 1934 election. In Missouri, a gunman killed a white man for helping black voters get to the polls. One man took the life of another during a fight at a polling place in Ohio. It was said they disagreed on the election. In Kentucky, a man tried to wrestle a gun away from his brother. The gun went off, and the brother died at the scene. In another Kentucky incident in which two opposing supporters quarreled over who deserved to win, a man was stabbed to death. Yet as tragic as these events were, the story that most captivated the nation was that of a small-town party boss who instigated the murder of five of his own neighbors.

Why did Joe Bruno and his family fire on unarmed parade marchers? The truth is a secret Joe took to the grave. Surely, it could not have been something as spontaneous as fear of an unruly mob. Were that the case, there would have been no waiting, loaded arsenal in his bedroom. And if the parade marchers were actually rioters in disguise and bent on violence, would they have put a truckload of children—who were near the head of the parade—directly in the cross hairs? But perhaps the biggest unanswered question is this: did Joe Bruno really believe he was going to get away with murder? Was his ego that large? Or did he believe he had enough men and women in his pocket to ensure he would walk away from any charges? If that's true, Joe made one major miscalculation. While politicians, judges and jurors might be swayed or cajoled, the people of Kelayres had had enough of "Big Joe." They were the wild card he likely never considered.

We can also only speculate about how Joe Bruno might have viewed his own escape from county prison. Was his plan to find a way to free the rest of his family once he was out? If so, where would they all go, and how could a group of such well-recognized men evade capture? Considering his purported plans to flee to South America, it seems unlikely he could have aided his kin from there. Or maybe he believed his family members were making their own escape plans. Perhaps he thought his brother Phil could fare prison life far better than he himself could. Maybe he believed his sons would obtain early releases—or that they were still young enough to rebuild their lives after serving their full sentences. Maybe he simply didn't care about anyone's condition other than his own. Whatever his post-escape plans (if any), like the motives behind the killing of five men, they were never revealed.

Unlike Joe, the other jailed Brunos looked to the men who prosecuted and jailed them for assistance with release. On April 8, 1937, the parents of Tony Orlando wrote to Lewis D. Buono, begging his aid:

> *We the parents of Toney* [sic] *Orlando take the advantage in asking your cooperation for help to seek Toney's freedom.*
>
> *You know as well as we and the people in his community that Toney is an innocent victim of circumstances.*
>
> *We are sure that your help would mean a lot of good so please do all within your power.*
>
> *Respectfully yours,*
> *Mr. and Mrs. Charles Orlando*

In 1940, Orlando's wife, Mildred, filed a third request with the board of pardons. Her plea was based on Orlando's trouble-free prison record and the fact that a home and job awaited his release.

James Bruno had no qualms about going above Buono's or the board of pardon's heads. In an undated letter written before his father's escape from the Schuylkill County Prison, James pleaded his case directly to Governor George H. Earle. If the time frame of its composition was not known, one might assume that James had been jailed for years and that he had no political loyalties whatsoever:

> *My Dear Governor;*
> *I wish that your Honorable Sir will give me about ten minutes of your most valuable time…I am at the present time* [incarcerated] *for a period of*

from 10 to 20 years, due to the result of the Kelayres tragedy of which you no doubt remember very well.

…I have been in prison since November 5, 1933 and it certainly has been a long time to me up until the present date. My purpose, Dear Governor, is will you please for the sake of a human life pardon me at your earliest convenience, because due to this terrible tragedy, I have lost a good position in life, my job, my home, my wife and my health is failing me badly, no one at home to take care of my poor mother and the remainder of my family who is a brother, 14 years of age. My younger brother and dad are in prison with me. Some people have told me that it would be useless to apply for a pardon under your administration because it is a Democratic one and the Brunos were Republicans.

I hope, Dear Governor, that that would not be the case…You have been an asset to the people of the good Commonwealth and you certainly would be a very good candidate for that great office of the president of these United States.

This tragedy, honorable sir, was merely an accident and I am innocent of what I have been accused of. In fact the men that were killed that night were all friends of mine. I hold no personal animosity against any of them and that is as true as there is a God in heaven.

…Please Governor, give me a chance in this world as I am still a young man and I know I can make good again if left go at this time.

I have never been arrested before in my life for any crime as I have been away to college and my associates were charges of the best families, you being a college man know that Governor.

I am of present a trusty in the warden's office of the Schuylkill County prison. As to my behavior, I refer you to the warden…
P.S. Please don't just throw this letter in the waste-basket. Will you kindly consider this young man's future. Thank you very much.

Paul Bruno was the only one of the original defendants to be granted a new trial and freed. Arthur served the second least amount of time, winning early parole in 1938. Tony Orlando was freed the year after his wife made her third plea for mercy. Alfred and James were paroled in 1942, and Phil was released a few years later.

Although many believed that several of the Schuylkill County commissioners aided the Bruno escape, in the end, no charges stuck. Lewis D. Buono himself made public his belief that these rumors were unfounded. At least half a dozen other individuals were charged with perjury, solicitation to commit perjury or being a material witness to a murder. Most of these cases simply vanished into the ether.

Joe Bruno served the longest sentence of any member of his family for the murders on election eve 1934. It was not until January 13, 1948, that "Big Joe" finally got the news he'd so long awaited. The memo from the parole board read:

> *Name: Joseph J. Bruno*
> *Number: D-2381*
> *The Board of Parole at the 1-12-48 meeting rendered the following decision in your case:*
> *Parole granted to be effective 1-17-48 or, at such time thereafter as you shall have an acceptable parole plan.*

Joe returned to his expensive home at the corner of Fourth and Centre Streets in Kelayres, but he wasn't welcomed by everyone. Paul Salidago recalls the day when he, a young boy at the time, answered a knock on the door of the family's brick two-story to find Joe Bruno standing before him.

"Is your dad home?" Joe asked.

"He is," Paul remembers saying, "and you better leave now."

On July 5, 1951, Joe was admitted to St. Joseph's Hospital in Hazleton. He had been ill for some weeks prior to admission. Five days later, Joe was dead. According to his death certificate, Joe died of congestive heart failure brought on by myocardial heart disease. His occupation—apparently provided by the informant, Joe's daughter Antoinette Billig—was listed as "politician." Cecelia Bruno, Joe's wife, died less than eight years later of a heart attack.

Joe's obituaries spoke little of any facts of his life outside of his part in the Kelayres Massacre, his trials and his incarceration. He would leave a legacy not as a public servant or philanthropist but rather as a common criminal.

While Joe Bruno's name was tarnished, Lewis D. Buono's star rose and shone ever brighter at the end of his life. Like Joe, it was Buono's heart that gave out on him. On December 1, 1954, Buono sat in the hospital waiting for an electrocardiogram. He died of a heart attack before he could be seen.

Unlike Joe's, Buono's obituaries were flowery tributes, with headlines like "Famous Detective Dies." The singular most inaccurate statement repeated in several versions of his obituary is a line describing Buono's single-handed arrest of "Big Joe" Bruno. It was a falsity that no doubt Buono himself would have been the first to correct.

Joseph J. Bruno's death certificate (for which information was provided by his loyal daughter Antoinette Billig). Joe's birth date was October 20, 1888—making him a full decade younger than he reported on his marriage license. Even in death, his occupation was listed as "politician." *From Pennsylvania Department of Health death certificates.*

Albert L. Thomas was also well remembered for his role in the Bruno trials. Thomas died in his Meadville, Crawford County home on May 9, 1942. The judge against whom he had run and about whom he had complained in his letter to Lewis Buono ordered all courts and law offices closed on the afternoon of Thomas's funeral. Meadville residents described it as one of the most-attended funerals in recent memory.

Charles J. Margiotti, attorney general under Governor George H. Earle, remained in politics and developed a reputation as a man who enjoyed his own press. Margiotti had survived three heart attacks before succumbing to their cumulative damage on August 25, 1956. He was sixty-five years old. In addition to his own claims that he was sole recipient of the tip that had precipitated the Bruno arrest, Margiotti's obituaries contained other boasts—one that he was largely responsible for Earle's historic 1934 win, a silly and unfounded statement considering the realities of that election.

Democrats took control of the state's House of Representatives in 1934. Governor Earle, as promised during his campaign, immediately began creating programs that would come to be called his "Little New Deal." Many of Earle's plans during his first two years, however, were blocked by the Republican-controlled senate. When, in November 1936, Democrats won both houses, Earle was able to advance his programs without opposition. Among legislation passed were the limiting of the workweek to forty hours, a minimum wage for women and minors, statewide oversight of "poor boards" and the merging of the state police with the mounted police.

In 1938, Margiotti announced his own bid for governor, a decision that pitted him against sitting governor and fellow Democrat Earle. As part of his campaign rhetoric, Margiotti promised to investigate what he described as the Earle administration's misuse of New Deal funds and programs. Earle fired Margiotti on the grounds that, while the attorney general had alleged bribery by state officials, he refused to present the evidence. It was a poorly kept secret, however, that the issues between Margiotti, Earle and the Democratic leadership were actually based on bruised political egos. The upshot of this feuding and infighting was the creation of a grand jury charged with investigating Margiotti's claims. The House of Representatives stepped in with a dictate that no investigation would occur before it could determine the validity of Margiotti's accusations. That investigation, the House said, proved the charges to be without merit.

Margiotti eventually dropped out of the gubernatorial race, but by then, the Democrats had wounded themselves so badly that there was no chance of recovery. As the Democrats had done in 1934, the Republicans won all contested state offices in 1938. Earle's fall was as furious as his rise, and after one term, he was out of office.

Republicans resided in the governor's mansion for the next four elections. Democrats won in 1954 and 1958. Since then, control of Pennsylvania has swung back and forth between the parties—circumstances that those who voted for George H. Earle in 1934 might never have imagined.

In the anthracite counties of Pennsylvania, production peaked in 1914. The very next year, the Harwood Electric Company received a ten-year contract to light the streets in the little village of Kelayres. No one would have guessed that this modern, convenient and relatively cheap power source would signal the beginning of the end of king coal and the livelihoods of so many who depended on it.

As for the most important people in this story—the victims—as if life weren't hard enough in Kelayres, it got only worse for their survivors. Susan Lis, granddaughter of William Forke, shares a story likely similar to what the other four families experienced. For her grandmother Mary, William's wife, memories of the massacre never really faded. "My grandmother didn't remarry until 1950," Susan says, "and only then because Catherine, her youngest daughter…refused to set a wedding date until her mother was remarried." A widower named Bart Stoll had met and quickly fallen in love with Mary. After some urging, she wed a second time. It was a happy union but all too brief. In 1953, Mary was widowed again. In 1957, Mary moved to New Jersey to live in the household of her daughter Theresa (Susan's mother).

Theresa passed away in 2007. "Going through her belongings after her death," recalls Susan, "I came across a copy of her father's death certificate. I knew all those years how my grandfather had died, but it wasn't until I saw the cause of death…a gunshot wound to the abdomen, that it really made me realize what my grandmother, mother, uncle and aunt actually went through back in 1934."

Chapter 16

AROUND IN A CIRCLE

If you were to follow the mailman on his route through Kelayres, you might be surprised to see some familiar names among his deliveries: Perna, McAloose, Salidago, Russo, Cara. There was nothing about the night of November 5, 1934, that made residents flee the little village, nor did it sour the opinions of families who had lived there for generations. Homes have passed down through several family members since the massacre, and life goes on with few surprises.

In 1994, Kline Township found itself embroiled in yet another election scandal. Frank J. Sacco, director of Schuylkill County's election bureau, was charged with ballot box tampering. It was alleged that he altered several dozen ballots cast in the general election of 1993. Specifically, the ballots of Democratic voters were changed to Republican votes in races for township supervisor and auditor. According to statements taken during the investigation, Sacco pulled guards from the ballot boxes in an effort to save the county the expense of their salaries. In what seems an amazing case of history repeating itself, Sacco's mother was a Forke. And leading the call for an investigation of the election was Andrew McAloose, Democratic chairman for Kline Township.

Sacco was found guilty of voter fraud and, in July 1994, was sentenced to six months of house arrest and fined $1,000. While under house arrest, Sacco felt compelled to participate in the special election precipitated by his own ballot tampering. He made campaign calls for Republican candidates—right up until the time members of the community complained that he was likely not the best man for that job.

The Bruno home today. The street signs show the deadly intersection where the Kelayres Massacre occurred on November 5, 1934. *Photograph taken by author.*

There are very few people in Kelayres who aren't in some way connected to one another or to the now nearly forgotten Kelayres Massacre. They freely share what they know, and they are matter-of-fact about its unyielding place in their village history.

These families are the best reasons to preserve the story of the murder of five men on election eve in 1934—not because of the Democratic landslide to which the massacre is wrongly attributed. And not because of the massacre's exaggerated connections to organized crime. The story of the Kelayres Massacre is, after all, just a story about people—about family and friends of the people who still live in Kelayres. Like any biographical record, it deserves to be saved for generations to come.

Across the street from what was once Joe Bruno's home and just down the way toward McAdoo stands a red brick, two-story building that has seen better days. If you look very, very closely at the frontispiece over the front door, you will see that the words "Kelayres" and "School" are of slightly different chiseled font. And you'll notice that the concrete into which the

The Kelayres School, originally built by Joe Bruno, was his pride and joy. Look closely at the sign today and you'll see that the word "Kelayres" is carved into newer stone than the word "School." The original stone bearing the name "Bruno" was removed after the massacre. *Photograph taken by author.*

word "Kelayres" is set is whiter—newer. This sign did not used to bear these anomalies, for when the school was originally built, the words emblazoned on that building read, "Bruno School." Like the man who named it after himself, the school is now gone, and only the vestiges of its once proud façade remain. Meanwhile, a new and modern facility serves the more than four hundred elementary-age children of Kelayres and McAdoo, none of whom knows or cares about Joe Bruno.

SOURCES

ARCHIVAL MATERIALS
Schuylkill County Historical Society

LETTERS:

James J. Bruno to Governor George Earle, undated.

Joseph J. Bruno to wife Cecelia, undated.

Lewis D. Buono to "Mr. J.A.," April 10, 1937.

L.E. Enterline to J.L. Hughes, August 26, 1937.

James A. Glenney to Lewis D. Buono, November 15, 1934.

Mr. and Mrs. Charles Orlando to Lewis D. Buono, April 8, 1937.

Arthur L. Thomas to H.O. Bechtel, July 17, 1935.

Arthur L. Thomas to James J. Gallagher, July 25, 1935.

Arthur L. Thomas to Lewis D. Buono, April 5, 1935.

Arthur L. Thomas to Lewis D. Buono, July 10, 1937.

Evidence tags from weapons and ammunition recovered from the crime scene.

Handwritten and typed case notes, Lewis D. Buono.

Handwritten statements from Wilbur Hale, Michael Kulish, Handel Tonkin and George Wallyung.

Inventory of Joseph J. Bruno's safety deposit box.

Police photos of crime scene, including interior of the home of Joseph J. Bruno.

Typed depositions, created by prosecution.

Wanted poster, created by the Pennsylvania State Police for Joseph J. Bruno (after escape).

Pennsylvania State Police Historical, Educational and Memorial Center

Evidence exhibits, including Mary Dvorak's shoe and stocking, a blood-spattered tie (owner unknown), a man's hat with blood and pellet holes (owner unknown but presumed to be William Forke), a piece of wood siding with pellet holes, a piece of window frame with an embedded bullet and an American flag with pellet holes.

Personnel file card collection.

Photographs of the original "Kelayres Massacre" display case.

Pennsylvania State Archives

Schuylkill County Criminal Sessions Records.

Vital Records (birth, marriage, death).

BOOKS

Bernard, Clyde. *Kelayres Massacre and History of Bruno Corruptible Political Reign.* N.p., n.d.

Catholic Standard and Times Almanac. Philadelphia: Catholic Standard and Times Publishing Co., 1916.

Dunaway, Wayland Fuller. *A History of Pennsylvania.* New York: Prentice-Hall, 1935.

Eighty-Fifth Annual Report of the Inspectors of the State Penitentiary for the Eastern District of Pennsylvania for the Year 1914. Philadelphia, 1915.

Fortenbaugh, Robert. *Pennsylvania: The Story of a Commonwealth.* Harrisburg: Pennsylvania Book Service, 1940.

Hammond's Handy Atlas of the World. New York: C.S. Hammond & Co., 1912.

Higby, Clinton D. *The Government of Pennsylvania and the Nation.* Boston: D.C. Heath & Co., 1909.

Mayo, Katherine. *Justice to All: The Story of the Pennsylvania State Police.* New York: Knickerbocker Press, 1917.

Report of the Superintendent of Common Schools of Pennsylvania. Harrisburg: Pennsylvania State Printer, 1893.

Schalck, Adolph W. *History of Schuylkill County, Pennsylvania.* Vols. 1, 2. Pennsylvania State Historical Association, 1907.

Second Annual Report of the Public Service Commission of the Commonwealth of Pennsylvania. Harrisburg: Pennsylvania State Printer, 1917.

Sharpless, Isaac. *Two Centuries of Pennsylvania History.* Philadelphia: J.B. Lippincott Co., 1900.

Shimmell, L.S. *A Short History of Pennsylvania.* New York: Charles E. Merrill Co., 1910.

Smith, Ernest Ashton. *Allegheny, A Century of Education, 1815–1915.* Meadville, PA: Allegheny College History Co., 1916.

Smull's Legislative Hand Book and Manual of the State of Pennsylvania. Harrisburg: Pennsylvania State Printer, 1918, 1933, 1934.

Wallace, Paul A.W. *Pennsylvania: Seed of a Nation.* New York: Harper & Row, 1962.

WPA Federal Art Project Photographs of Pennsylvania Coal Miners and Coal Mining Communities. Jack Delano, photographer. Ca. 1938.

NEWSPAPERS

Space constraints prohibit the listing of every article consulted during the course of researching this book. Suffice it to say, however, that the contextual details offered by these stories provided a vital understanding of the Kelayres Massacre and subsequent events. What follows is a list of Pennsylvania newspapers carrying pertinent coverage:

Altoona Mirror

Chester Times

Clearfield Progress

Franklin News Herald

Gettysburg Times

Greenville Record Argus

Harrisburg Daily News Record

Harrisburg Telegraph

Hazleton Plain Speaker

Hazleton Standard-Speaker

Huntingdon Daily News

Indiana Evening Gazette

Kane Republican

Lebanon Daily News

Lehigh Valley Morning Call

Lock Haven Express

New Castle News

Oil City Blizzard

Pittsburgh Press

Pittston Gazette

Titusville Herald

Tyrone Daily Herald

Uniontown Morning Herald

Wilkes-Barre Evening News

Wilkes-Barre Sunday Independent

Regional New York newspapers with coverage of the events include:

Brooklyn Daily Eagle

Cornell Daily Sun

Jamestown Post-Journal

Wellsville Daily Reporter

Publications of a national scope that reported on the Kelayres Massacre and aftermath include:

New York Times

Time magazine

MISCELLANEOUS RESOURCES

Federal Census, Schuylkill County, Kline Township.

Schuylkill County deed and property tax records.

World War I and World War II draft registration cards.

Index

A

Adams, Lynn G. 22, 52, 98
Anthracite Strike Commission 20

B

Bechtel, H.O. 76, 113
Bevanko, Michael 71
Billig, Antoinette Bruno 31, 42, 62, 76,
    83, 86, 89, 92, 95, 104, 105
Bonnie and Clyde 63
bootlegging 23, 26, 28
Bruno, Alfred 31, 42, 49, 78, 89, 103
Bruno, Arthur 49, 62, 77, 78, 84
Bruno, Cecelia Rizzuto 30, 31, 49, 71,
    72, 73, 89, 97, 104, 113
Bruno, Elveda 31, 35, 36, 49
Bruno, Ernest 10, 31, 115
Bruno, Frank 29
Bruno, James 102, 103
Bruno, James (son of Joseph J. Bruno)
    29, 31, 33, 41, 42, 49, 53, 62,
    67, 70, 71, 77, 78, 87, 89, 113
Bruno, Joseph J. 9, 10, 14, 28, 30, 31,
    33, 35, 36, 38, 40, 41, 42, 43,
    47, 49, 53, 59, 61, 62, 63, 65,
    66, 67, 68, 69, 70, 71, 72, 73,
    74, 75, 76, 77, 78, 80, 82, 83,
    84, 86, 87, 89, 90, 91, 92, 93,
    95, 96, 97, 98, 99, 100, 102,
    104, 110, 111, 113, 114
Bruno, Louis 33
Bruno, Lucy 49
Bruno, Paul 9, 31, 41, 45, 47, 49, 77,
    78, 103
Bruno, Peter 29
Bruno, Phil 102
Bruno, Philip 14, 30, 33, 35, 42, 49,
    52, 62, 67, 69, 76, 77, 78, 79,
    83, 84, 103
Buono, Evangelista 79
Buono, Felice 79
Buono, Lewis D. 10, 11, 65, 66, 70, 77,
    79, 80, 81, 82, 84, 87, 89, 91,
    93, 95, 96, 97, 98, 99, 102, 103,
    104, 105, 113, 114

C

Cara, Elizabeth 33
Cara, Joseph 44
Cara, Mildred 71, 76
Carr, John A. 70

Cesario, Emil 70
Chevinsky, William 76
Christ, Harry F. 70
Church of the Immaculate Conception
31, 41, 42, 44, 57
Civilian Conservation Corps 40
Coal and Iron Police 19, 20, 21
Connors, Mrs. John 74
Cuba 97, 98

D

Daily, John 47
Daubert, Ervin 75
Delano, Jack 23
DeMario, Joseph 43
Dino, Jennie 44
Dino, Rose 44
Dolan, James 42
Dvorak, Mary 44, 45, 114

E

Earle, George H. 23, 55, 56, 58, 89,
102, 105, 106, 113
Ehrig, Phil 83, 84, 91, 92
Enterline, L.E. 87, 100, 113

F

Farmer, Charlese 11
Fenton, Mary 11
Festa, Ben 76
Fiorella, Frank 41, 44, 57, 66, 69, 70,
71, 74, 76
Fiorella, Samuel 70
Forke, Catherine 107
Forke family 109
Forke, Mary 107
Forke, Theresa 57, 107
Forke, William 44, 57, 76, 77, 78,
107, 114
Francis, William W. 70
Fudge, Beatrice 69

G

Gallagher, James J. 65, 71, 76, 95, 113
Gallagher, Joseph L. 38
Galosky, John 44, 75, 76
gambling 26, 28
Garramone, Rocco 98
Glenney, James A. 81, 113
Golden, Bill 87
Gosselin, Herbert F. 83, 84, 86, 87, 89,
91, 92, 97
Gowan, Felix R. 70
Grego, Mrs. Charles 42
Griffiths, Edwin 70
Groome, John C. 21
Guffy, Joseph F. 55

H

Hale, Kathy 11
Hale, Wilbur 84, 86, 114
Harwood Electric Company 106
Hauptmann, Bruno 63
Hicks, Roy B. 92
Holly 31
Holton, Jack 87
Honeybrook 18, 29, 30
Hoover, Herbert 17
Hughes, J.L. 113

I

Irving, Guy 84, 86, 87, 91, 92, 97

J

Jeansville 31
Jones, Benjamin R. 10, 75, 76, 77

K

Kalbach, Robert 92
KDKA 63
Kennedy, Thomas 56
Kline Township 14, 18, 26, 29, 30, 36,
38, 40, 53
Kordish, Stanley 43
Kostishion, Andrew 44, 57, 75, 76

Kostishion, Anna 57
Kulish, Michael 71, 114

L

Lenker, John F. 70
Lesko, Julia 49
Lindbergh, Charles 63
Lis, Susan 107

M

Margiotti, Charles J. 55, 58, 65, 74, 76, 77, 89, 91, 92, 93, 95, 99, 105, 106
Mascarelli, Sam 69
Maurer, Alvin 84, 91, 92
Mayo, Katherine 21
McAdoo 29, 30, 31, 40, 53, 58, 110, 111
McAdoo Heights 37
McAloose, Andrew 109
McAloose, Carl 37
McAloose, Dan 37, 41
McAloose Family 33, 37, 76
McAloose, John 37, 42
McAloose, Joseph 37
McAloose, Louis 37
McAloose, Madaline 37
McDonald, Anna 38
Memmi, Thomas 10
Minor, William 38
Mollie Maguires 59
Motika, Deborah Bruno 10, 35, 36

N

National Guard 20
Nilo, Joshua 98

O

Orlando, Charles 113
Orlando, Mildred 102
Orlando, Tony 42, 62, 71, 78, 83, 84, 102, 103

P

Palmer, Cyrus 67, 68, 74
Payer, Adolph 43
Pennsylvania Daily Packet and Advertiser 63
Pennsylvania State Police 10, 18, 19, 28, 38, 45, 46, 47, 48, 52, 69, 70, 114
Pennypacker, Samuel W. 20
Perna, Dominic 44, 57, 69, 75, 76, 78
Perna, Nicholas 41
Pinchot, Gifford 21, 52
Pinkerton, Allan 19
Pinkerton Detective Agency 19
Prohibition 17
Public Works Administration 40

R

Roosevelt, Franklin Delano 14, 17, 40, 53
Roosevelt, Theodore 19, 20
Rundell, Leonard 80
Russo, Peter 49

S

Sacco, Frank J. 109
Salidago drugstore 41, 58
Salidago, John 31, 45
Salidago, Paul 10, 104
Sauer, George M. 70
Schmoyer, horse thief 79, 80
Schnader, William A. 52, 65
Schuylkill County Historical Society 11
Shenandoah, Schuylkill County 20
Silverbrook 18, 29
slot machine 26
Smith, Harvey J. 79, 84
Social Security 40
Socker, Eva 49
state hospital 18
Stetler, Christina 11
Stevens, John B. 68
Stoll, Bart 107
Straka, Cecelia 49
Stramara, Sammy 61, 62

T

Taylor, M. Harvey 40, 52, 53
Thomas, Albert L. 65, 66, 68, 69, 70,
        75, 76, 77, 105, 113
Tonkin, Handel 86, 114
Tortanessi, Jenni 69, 71
Trella, Lucille 9, 36
Treskow 31

U

United Mine Workers 20, 57

V

Vacater, Carl 42
Vendura, Mildred 44
Vespucci, Edward 45
Volstead Act 28

W

Walker, Robert 84, 87, 97
Wallyung, George 84, 87, 114
Watkins, G. Harold 38
Wishnefski, Annie 72

Z

Zapach, Sergeant Jeffery D. 10

About the Author

The Kelayres Massacre: Politics & Murder in Pennsylvania's Anthracite Coal Country is Stephanie's third book for The History Press. Like its two predecessors, *The Killing of John Sharpless* and *Philadelphia Spiritualism and the Curious Case of Katie King*, it stems from Stephanie's interest in historical true crimes and the interesting characters who commit them.

Stephanie's professional writing career began when she was hired as a stringer by the long-defunct *Pennsylvania Beacon*. Since that time, she has amassed more than two hundred bylines in local, regional and national publications and cultivated a reputation as a Pennsylvania research specialist. She has been called on for both on-air and behind-the-scenes work by the Travel Channel, NBC's *Who Do You Think You Are*, PBS's *Finding Your Roots* and Canada's *Ancestors in the Attic*, among others.

A lifelong Pennsylvania resident born within smelling distance of the Hershey Chocolate Factory, Stephanie lives in the Capital Region of the state with her husband, two dogs and two cats (the brains of the operation). Stephanie now writes full time, and in October 2014, she fulfilled a lifetime dream by launching *Prose 'n Cons*™—a quarterly magazine devoted to the mystery, crime and suspense genres. To learn more about Stephanie's books, magazine or other projects, visit StephanieHoover.com or Prose-n-Cons.com.